PRACTI  ...AGOGY

Theories, values and tools to
with children and young

Jan Storø

First published in Great Britain in 2013 by

The Policy Press
University of Bristol
Fourth Floor
Beacon House
Queen's Road
Bristol BS8 1QU
UK
Tel +44 (0)117 331 4054
Fax +44 (0)117 331 4093
e-mail tpp-info@bristol.ac.uk
www.policypress.co.uk

North American office:
The Policy Press
c/o The University of Chicago Press
1427 East 60th Street
Chicago, IL 60637, USA
t: +1 773 702 7700
f: +1 773-702-9756
e:sales@press.uchicago.edu
www.press.uchicago.edu

British Library Cataloguing in Publication Data
A catalogue record for this book is available from the British Library.

Library of Congress Cataloging-in-Publication Data
A catalog record for this book has been requested.

ISBN 978 1 44730 538 5 paperback
ISBN 978 1 44730 539 2 hardcover

The right of Jan Storø to be identified as author of this work has been asserted by him in accordance with the 1988 Copyright, Designs and Patents Act.

Cover design by thecoverfactory
Front cover: image kindly supplied by www.istock.com
Printed and bound in Great Britain by TJ International, Padstow
The Policy Press uses environmentally responsible print partners

Contents

Preface to the original Norwegian edition

It may be useful for the reader to know something about my starting point for writing this book, as it affects some of the more technical discussions I describe. As you read, you will see that social pedagogy straddles the domains of theory and practice. The practical part has one foot in various types of change-oriented and environmental, or milieu therapy with children and young people, while the other is immersed in the application of the law and in the administration of casework. I want to say something about my own position in these fields.

I worked for many years in the child welfare field, first and foremost in residential care. This places me more firmly in a practical than a theoretical domain. It is, therefore, not surprising that I write about the practising element of social pedagogy, as this is where my main experience lies. However, over the past few years, my interest in understanding what is happening on a higher theoretical level has increased. This led to a Master's degree in social work, and subsequently to a teaching position as associate professor in the Faculty of Social Sciences at Oslo and Akershus University College of Applied Sciences. That makes me a practitioner who has directed his gaze towards the theoretical field, towards academia. I have experienced the inherent duality of social pedagogy as a professional field.

The other particular feature of my experience is that I have worked far more in residential care where I have encountered children and young people struggling with their lives than I have been involved in the administration of casework. My version of practical social pedagogy is, therefore, more oriented towards change-oriented and *milieu* work than towards the child welfare pedagogue's casework in the child welfare services. I have, of course, tried to take this into consideration while writing, so that the book does not end up dealing only with *milieu* work.

During the work on the book, I used both books and articles and a fundamental understanding gained through contact over many years with two of my professional mentors: Erik Grønvold and Erik Larsen. I have used Erik Grønvold as a conversation partner during the work on the book, and he has generously shared his knowledge of social pedagogy with me during our many discussions. I have also learnt a lot from teaching alongside him. Erik Larsen is mostly represented in the book through my use of some of his professional ideas as expressed in his books and articles, but also through our conversations. Erik Larsen has a *psychological* eye on the work with children and young people, and he writes mostly about milieu therapy. I have, in other words, pulled out elements of this thinking and used them as building blocks in my own attempt at describing a *pedagogically* oriented practice. I am wholly responsible for such use. A big thank you to Erik and Erik.

Some of the material has been developed in dialogue with Jan Tesli Stokke in connection with our seminars for institution personnel in North West Russia over several years. I have learnt a lot about social pedagogy through this, and am grateful both to him and the seminar participants.

As I have included much of my own experience in the material, I ought to mention two of my previous workplaces: Frydenberg Residential Youth Centre in the late 1970s and early 1980s, and Grepperød Child Welfare Centre in the 1990s. These two in particular have been my arenas of experience.

Many people deserve thanks for their help with the writing process. My boss during the period when I started the work, the then Head of Studies Åse Broman, and my boss when I completed the work, Head of Studies Eva Bertling Herberg, have both contributed by generously allowing me to make time for writing. The Norwegian Union of Social Educators and Social Workers (FO) has provided me with a grant in order to finance the writing period, as did my previous employer, the Department of Social Work at Oslo University College. These two sources of finance have been vital in order to complete the book.

Several people have read through parts or all of the manuscript in order to give feedback, corrections and advice. Such help is invaluable to an author. Anne Jansen and Erik Grønvold, in particular, have contributed much excellent input and many discussions. Benny Lihme has also read my material, and his feedback has been very useful. In addition, Stein Himsett, Amelie Fougner and Åse Broman have provided excellent contributions after reading different versions of the manuscript along the way. It has also given me great pleasure to read parts of Roger Mathiesen's own manuscript (Mathiesen, 2008), and have discussions with him.

Moss / Oslo
updated 10 December 2012
JS

Preface to the English edition

Discussion of social pedagogy in Norway is often prefaced by describing the foundation of the study of social pedagogy at the University of Oslo in 1975. According to Jæger Sivertsen and Kvaran (2006) the Oslo approach to the study of pedagogy and education was more sociological: characterised by an orientation towards society and with a more radical profile. Today in Norway only professional education for the 'barnevernpedagog' (child welfare pedagogue) can be said to rest fully on social pedagogic grounds. The Norwegian Ministry's General Plan for barnevernpedagog education (heter det) states that 'Child welfare pedagogue education in Norway is a social work education directed towards children and young people. Social pedagogy work is the term for this professional practice' (Kunnskapsdepartementet, 2005).

This book was originally written to explore and explain contemporary social pedagogy. I became tired of the never-ending discussions, and the complaint that it is too difficult to define the practice and theory of social pedagogy. I wanted to contribute – not to more open-ended discussions – but to more clarity. It seemed to me that the connection between theory and practice within social pedagogy is a crucial topic. As I try to demonstrate from the very start of the book, we could perhaps talk about a crisis in the relationship between theory and practice within this field; an idea that I have developed further in a recent article (Storø, 2012).

Working with children and young people is a fascinating field. The complexity of this area of practice makes it interesting but also difficult. Over the past few years I have travelled and met colleagues in many countries, in different cultures. It strikes me that many of the ideas for working with children and young people are comparable, if not similar. The differences are mostly connected to legislation and to cultural traditions within the professions. But these differences are often overshadowed by a deeply rooted will to practise 'in the best interests of the child', with the result that professionals from different countries and cultures often will find that they have a common language for what they do, and for how they talk about what they do. This has inspired me to seek out dialogue with colleagues in other contexts. Publishing this book in English provides me with the opportunity to open that dialogue internationally. I also believe that the social pedagogy tradition in Norway, as distinct from the tradition in other countries, can be of interest to and value for colleagues internationally.

Moss/Oslo
10 December 2012
JS

This translation has been published with the financial support of NORLA.

CHAPTER ONE

Introduction – why social pedagogy?

Social pedagogy is a concept that is used in several different professional connections, which can be understood in many different ways. *My* starting point is that it constitutes a perspective for working with people with different problems, with its main focus on children and young people. Other Norwegian language literature about social pedagogy deals mainly with underlying theoretical issues and, to a much lesser extent, with social pedagogic practice. Students training to become child welfare pedagogues, but also others with similar training, need literature that will widen this picture. This book is intended as a basic text on the more *practical aspect* of social pedagogic practice. In his book of 1979, Ivar Frønes writes about social learning in a way that is parallel to what this professional practice is about. He writes that 'It is training in, participation in and understanding of social life. Not in any deep, therapeutic way, but in terms of skills for the participation in various social contexts, the ability to master different situations' (Frønes, 1979, p 36).

I have written this book in order to try to find a link between the practice and the theory that together shape the social pedagogue's professional reality.[1] I wanted to investigate what this practice and theory might be able to achieve together. No occupational group in Norway has appropriated the professional title of 'social pedagogue', and the concept is thus 'available' to those who want to claim it. It is also partly open to those who want to define it. This book is a forum for such attempts at a definition. The title of the book hints at such an attempt. It states that this practice is about what you do. At the same time, you will be reading that social pedagogic action is not arbitrary. It has to be constructed on theory, *and* be connected to specific professional values. Only then can we talk about *professional* actions, about an informed practice.

Let us meet Trond and Mette. They happen to be sitting next to each other in a crowded lunchtime cafe. Trond notices that Mette is reading a book called *Social pedagogic perspectives*. He thinks: "I'd like to meet her, and this is a way to start a conversation".

"Hi, what are you reading?"

Mette looks up. The man next to her leans towards her, alluding casually to the book she is absorbed in.

"What, this? Well, it's about social pedagogy. You probably think it's a bit of a weird subject. On a hot summer's day, I mean."

Mette smiles at him and returns to the book, thinking: "I can't be bothered to chat, I really want to look through this new book. I've finally managed to get out of the office to get some peace, and now someone is trying to disturb me here as well."

"Actually, you're wrong."

Trond doesn't give up easily. Mette looks up and sighs.

"What do you mean?"

"I mean you're wrong. I don't think it's weird at all. You see, I caught a glimpse of the title of the book, that's why I said hello. We are practically colleagues."

Trond smiles cheekily and lifts his coffee glass in a 'toast' to Mette.

"I see. What makes you think that?"

Trond leans over towards the neighbouring table.

"Actually, I'm a social pedagogue. Quite simply. And if that's what you are too, then we are sort of colleagues. So we could have a coffee together, as colleagues do."

Mette understands that this is not the right place to look at her book, and she puts it away. She decides to drink the rest of her coffee with the enthusiastic 'colleague', and to try to find somewhere else to look at the book later. No point in getting upset about being interrupted on a day like this.

"OK, so tell me: if we are colleagues, where do you work?"

"I work with young people in outreach teams, here in the town. I've been doing it for many years. Some of the worst young drug addicts are my clients. I particularly work with this group because several of the people I work with would rather not have too much to do with those who are that far gone. But, personally, I like them. Do you have experience from outreach?"

Mette shifts in her chair.

"I'm not so sure that we are colleagues after all. You are right that I am a social pedagogue. But I don't work with young people. Nor with children."

"Really? Tell me more."

"Right, well, I understand that you use the same professional title as me, but we are actually working on completely different things. I'm a writer. Right now I am sitting here leafing through my new book. Published today. Hot off the press. So you see, my type of social pedagogy isn't the same as yours."

"OK … so you're a writer?! A woman with her head screwed on the right way, obviously. Impressive. May I have a look?"

Trond leans over towards the book, and takes it when he sees that Mette is not resisting.

"*Social Pedagogic Perspectives*. By Mette Grevstad. Great photo on the back!"

Trond holds the book up to Mette, and smiles while looking from her to the photo and back again.

"Really impressive. I'm Trond Frantsen."

"Hello, Trond Frantsen."

Mette smiles and extends a hand.

"Tell me what you write about."

Mette decides to give her conversation partner something to chew on.

"OK, the book is an attempt to understand the social pedagogic perspective in a contemporary context. I am particularly focusing on various marginalisation processes in post-modern society connected to the development of new media, with emphasis on the tools that are available to schools in order to promote integration and inclusion processes."

"Wow. That's quite something."

Trond leans back with a hesitant smile.

"Listen, maybe we are not colleagues after all."

Social pedagogy as work with people; social pedagogy as a theoretical perspective. Or, formulated slightly differently: on the one hand, an orientation towards clients with problems; on the other, an orientation towards science. We are beginning to sense the essence of the greatest confusion when trying to understand this concept. Maybe the conversation between Mette and Trond will develop in such a way that they arrive at a common frame of reference. Maybe they will be able to have a professional conversation with starting points in their quite different perspectives, nodding in recognition at the various terms they are using in their everyday lives. Maybe they can, but it is by no means certain.

I will, as early as Chapter Two, try to throw some light on the question of what social pedagogy actually is. As we have seen, there is no easy answer to this. The topic is constantly discussed among professionals with an interest in the fundamental questions about social pedagogy. It is not my aim to give you the final answers to the questions I pose, mainly because I believe that there are few final answers in this field. Social pedagogic theory and practice are areas that have to be created and recreated in the various contexts in which they are used. Therefore, one of the most important areas of competence for the social pedagogue is linked to the ability to analyse and reflect.

I have used a broad brush to define the social pedagogic arena. I am using the concept 'social pedagogic practice' about work in a wide range of situations where clients meet helpers. I can see no reason to limit this broad understanding. It is the content of what is practised, not the places where the practice is carried out, that determines what it is.

Non-pedagogic?

As a rule, a field of practice is characterised by clear norms and methods, and by weighty specialist theory. Normally, these will provide relatively comprehensible answers to difficult questions in the field. However, the social pedagogic field of practice is not quite like that. It is not a distinct field, and there are not that many easily available answers.

At the same time there is a lot to say about this field. Otherwise, there would be no point in writing this book. Pedagogy, or education, is about learning and the process of learning. This implies that social pedagogy must be about learning in social situations. But not everyone can see what is pedagogic in everyday social situations. It seems one has to be somewhat pedagogically oriented to focus on the learning aspect in all the *ordinary situations* when people come together.

> Ruby and Rigmor each have a 15-year-old son. One day, they are discussing their sons and their messy rooms. Ruby feels it is important that she, as a mother, should not go in and tidy up after her son. She hopes that he will learn to tidy up when he sees the consequences of all the mess. Rigmor, on the other hand, is happy to tidy up after her son when he is not at home. For her, it is important that the room is clean and tidy. She says to Ruby: "You are always so pedagogic. Can't you just do what is necessary?". But Ruby is adamant: "No way, I am NOT tidying up. Otherwise he will learn that it is fine not to do it himself."

It is not obvious who of these two is right. What is clear is that one is more preoccupied with learning than the other. For Rigmor, it is wrong to be 'pedagogic' in a situation like this. For Ruby, it is unthinkable to ignore the boy's responsibility for doing things at home.

Read the dialogue between Ruby and Rigmor one more time. Imagine this time that they are colleagues at a residential youth centre, and that they are talking about two of the young people who live there. Does the dialogue change when it is moved to a different context? As milieu therapists, they are both defined by a social pedagogic role. They are *supposed* to think pedagogically. But Rigmor's arguments can still be regarded as useful points of view in the discussion.

The social pedagogic field of practice is *sometimes* characterised by the paradox that what *appears* to be professionally the right thing to do isn't right at all. One source of error may be found precisely in the pedagogic perspective on everyday situations. Sometimes, the pedagogic needs to be toned down and something else toned up. It may be that the interpersonal relationship between helper and client becomes more important than learning and teaching. Social pedagogic relationships are always social in the sense that the helper and the one needing help find themselves together in such situations. The question is whether they are always pedagogic. It may be worthwhile to say that trying to be 'non-pedagogic' occasionally can be a good kind of social pedagogy. General collaboration between people in everyday situations consists of much more than learning, even when one person is a social pedagogue and the other a client. This implies that the social pedagogue needs to make sure that the learning aspect is included in the social situation. More often than not, we find this in the normal interaction between parents and children. Parents are always pedagogues in the sense that they bring up their children. But that does not mean that parents are *only* pedagogues, they are also carers, they play with their children, they spend time together without any other purpose than having a good time. It is exactly in such situations that the social pedagogic element – upbringing – is present in the ordinary and everyday.

It may sound as if I am saying that being pedagogic is contrary to being human. Let me emphasise strongly that this is not what I mean. In my effort to understand a social pedagogy that is human, I have reached the conclusion that pedagogy is important to people. But it isn't 'everything'. There is an inherent danger in pedagogic practice, namely, that the pedagogic element overshadows the general. We must remember that, as a rule, the pedagogue, or someone with a pedagogic orientation, is an administrator of power. This may be because the person in question has power in his role as an educator, as is the case with milieu therapists for example. Or it may be because the pedagogue, by definition, has the power to control others because they 'need to learn'. We need to be on our guard against this.

So, pedagogy is not contrary to being human and ordinary. Let me put it like this: luckily, pedagogy has the strength to allow us to scrutinise it on a more general, human level. However, we can only do this by being alert. Making ethics a companion to our everyday practice contributes to such alertness. In other words, the social pedagogue must always include a critical perspective on his own practice, as it happens. He must always be willing to submit the central professional principle – pedagogy – to potential criticism.

I would already here, in the very first chapter, like to emphasise that I think social pedagogy is an exciting perspective. I think social pedagogy is important. However, inherent in 'the pedagogic' is also the possibility of limiting general situations between people to only being about learning. As I see it, the best social pedagogue has both an eye on the pedagogic and a fingertip sensation for situations when the pedagogic view becomes too narrow, and additional views are required.

About terminology

I am using certain terms that I will explain as I go along. However, I would like to hone in on a few of them already here in the introduction. Our choice of terms is not arbitrary. We are guided by various preferences when using one particular term over another, without necessarily being aware of the factors that influence us. That is precisely why it is important to try to be conscious of our use of terms. Language, and therefore also terms, is a particularly important component of social pedagogic work. I will return to this in Chapter Seven, which deals with the social pedagogue's working tools.

Some of the terms I use are more complex than expressed by me in this book. This means that some readers may feel that my explanations are too simple. In the main, I do not write for those who want to delve deeply into these terms, but rather for people who need to become familiar with them. I hope that this will be a way into a world of terms that is useful in a practising social pedagogue's professional everyday life, and also provide an interest in delving deeper into the terms at a later stage.

Social pedagogue

When I write about the social pedagogue in this book, I mean the practising, actively engaged social pedagogue.[2] In Chapter Two, I will throw some light on what is meant by what I call the practising element of social pedagogy. In other words, I am not using the concept 'social pedagogue' about the professionals who mainly use social pedagogy as an analytical tool. There is obviously no clear border between these two ways of understanding the term 'social pedagogue', and it is therefore not always easy to spot. The practising social pedagogue also uses social pedagogic analysis and theories taken from social pedagogic academia.

As I see it, the difference between the analytical and the practising social pedagogue is that the first is a professional who, in the main, is a theorist, and the other is a professional who, in the main, is a practitioner. To the former, theory and politics are important, while the latter works in the everyday arenas of his clients. The former is interested in society and larger population groups; the latter turns his professional focus on individuals and small groups, and carries out practical work to bring about change in their lives.

The subtitle of the original, Norwegian edition of the book was *It is all about what you do*. It may look as if what I want is an individualised practice. I do not. My intention with the original subtitle was to show that action is important, that social pedagogic practice has to be measured against what the social pedagogue actually does. Most social pedagogues practise in a group of professionals where the group has joint responsibility for the actions taken. One of the main points I make in this book is that actions must be guided by values and grounded in theory, and thus not initiated solely by spontaneous and private reasoning. My ideal will always be a thoroughly reasoned practice where the social pedagogue collaborates with others – not least with the client. The *you* in the subtitle is there to try to establish a dialogue with individual social pedagogues and individual students who are training to become social pedagogic practitioners. The title of the book invites you to develop your own professionalism, practice and understanding – precisely to avoid individualising what you do. Because the social pedagogic person is interwoven with practice to such an extent, he needs to start working on himself right from day one.[3]

Client

As the main term for the person at the receiving end of the social pedagogue's work, I am using 'client'.[4] In this respect, I have made the same choice as Skau (2003), who is using the 'client' concept as a collective term. There is a need for one main concept to describe those receiving help in a book such as this. Clarity in the text is a weighty argument for this. I would nevertheless remind readers that the 'client' concept is controversial. Some feel it is old-fashioned and expressing a top-down attitude to those receiving help. However, I feel it is possible to use it loaded with values other than those traditionally associated with it. That is how I want to understand the 'client' concept in this book. We should also remember that the suggested alternatives are not entirely without problems. Of the new terms, the most frequently used in the last few years is 'service user'. This concept appears to solve some of the problems I mentioned, but it also raises new ones (Storø, 2003).

I want to make it clear that I view the client as an active participant in change-oriented work, which is a prerequisite for social pedagogic practice – this also goes for situations where there is no social pedagogue present. The client should be clearly understood as a subject, both in encounters with the social pedagogue and in his own life. Parton and O'Byrne (2000, p 9) make a similar choice in the use of terms, and, at the same time, choose to make a strong case for 'a client-centred approach'. There are two reasons for the authors' arguments. One is the ethical dimension, which implies treating the client well. The other is no less interesting. It implies the assumption that the opportunity for change is to be found within the client himself. The client does not need help to become another person, but to find new ways to describe himself. In this context, it is not sufficient to thematise the *client's contribution*. The client's life story is the real arena for the work towards change.

Change

The concept 'change' is used a lot in the book. Practical social pedagogic work is about creating change in people's lives. You could say that 'change' is a fundamental concept. Out in the field, there are also several other terms that encompass some of the same meaning. We are always hearing about treatment, developmental work, care or care work, milieu work, milieu therapy, and so on. In this book, I am using the term 'change' as a first choice, because it is sufficiently broad to apply to several different professions. The term is further developed in Chapter Five.

Intervention

The term 'intervention' refers to what the social pedagogue *does*, to the practice that he carries out. In some places, I write about *initiatives*, but to me that term points more in the direction of the intervention of an official. The social pedagogue practitioner is, of course, an official in terms of his appointment, but often also a person close to the client through their relationship in contexts resembling everyday life. For this reason, I prefer the somewhat broader term 'intervention'. Regardless of which one of these is used, it will refer to the active, practising element. Madsen (2006, p 220) writes that 'social pedagogic practice is based on visible intervention in other people's lives in order to create development, participation and learning'. This is the core activity of the social pedagogy practitioner.

The choice of the term 'intervention' may be criticised, partly for the same reasons as for the term 'client'. When we talk about intervention, it is easy to think of the client as passive. My reason for choosing to use it is therefore similar to the reasoning I used about the 'client' concept. First, it is necessary to have a main term for what the social pedagogue does. When we talk about the social pedagogy practitioner, we need to be able to describe this practice in a simple way. I also want to make it very clear that I do not see the term as pointing in the direction of a passive client who is subjected to the social pedagogue's practice. I am assuming that interventions chiefly contain invitations to collaboration and cooperation with clients, and that they are carried out in such a way that there is a demand for *the active client*. Addressing the client with a question about what he, himself, thinks, may be seen as an intervention in itself. Not least because we can then see that interventions in social pedagogic practice often occur in the form of language.

How to use this book

I recommend reading the book chapter by chapter, consecutively. The main reason for this is that things that are explained along the way are taken as understood later in the text.

In some places, I have devoted limited space to topics that may seem very important. One such example would be *communication*. If I had written extensively about communication, this book might have been twice as big. Besides, others have written more effectively about communication than I could. The general literature about communication is better suited to delving deeper into this area of social pedagogic competence.

Another example is *ethics*. Social pedagogic practice is moral through and through. With that, I mean that everything the social pedagogue does can, and should, be thoroughly investigated to check if the practice is ethically viable. It has been important to me to mention the ethical perspective here and there in the text; however, I have not aimed at a complete review of ethics in social pedagogic practice. For that, I refer to the general literature on ethics.

Construction

In this section, I will briefly introduce social constructionism, which I understand as a useful theoretical perspective in social pedagogic theory and practice. Briefly, a construction perspective on human activity implies thinking along the lines that people construct understanding in their practical realities. According to Burr (2003), such construction processes are social in that we collaborate and exchange experiences with each other when we construct understanding. This implies that looking for ultimate truths is not very relevant. What is 'true' for one person may not be true for another. This view may be seen as an alternative to a positivistic view that emphasises the search for what is exact and demonstrable. We could say that constructing is fitting together bits of the jigsaw to make a complete picture, or at least to make a picture we think is complete *enough*. We create what we might call a meaningful totality. When we join the pieces to form an overall understanding, we interpret what we see. Interpretations are also constructions. A scientific theoretical term for interpretation is 'hermeneutics'. Social pedagogy and social constructionism thus lie within a hermeneutic scientific tradition.

We see from this that in the type of professional perspective of which social pedagogy is an example, there are no completely distinct truths. We must, therefore, make a selection of assumptions and put them together to form a perspective that is as complete as possible, a perspective that we regard as useful. This is what I call a construction.

Thinking in terms of constructions has its advantages. It means that we can use our experiences, view them in relation to what we ourselves understand, connect them with what we learn from others, and create something qualitatively new, which we can personally vouch for. Thinking in constructions also gives us the opportunity to *reconstruct* when we feel it necessary. We can also renew and develop our own assumptions, thus creating fresh opportunities for action. New constructions give us the opportunity to go beyond experiences we would otherwise have. Another advantage of a construction perspective is that we can develop a constant search for new ways to tackle a problem. While working on this book, a friend told me that her old chemistry teacher had opened her eyes to constructions by saying: "This is how we understand it today, but it is not necessarily how we will understand it tomorrow". A wise teacher. Even within the practice of natural science, where one often seeks knowledge that is as certain and complete as possible, he was open to the possibility of a different way of looking at things. In social pedagogy, which has its origins in the social sciences, it is more obvious that there must be room for different versions of reality. In this field, it is rarely meaningful to talk about one kind of reality; it makes more sense to talk about different constructions.

I have now shown my true colours, and declared that I am working on this book within a social constructionist perspective. That means having a fundamental respect for the view that there are many different ways of looking at things, making decisions and taking action. What is best is by no means certain until we have actually tried it. Such a perspective needs to be accompanied by an investigative attitude. We need wonderment as a constant companion, and we must dare to submit our work to questioning: 'Does it work well?', 'For whom?', 'Are we achieving what we want?', 'What is the outcome of our efforts?', 'Have the lives of the people we worked with improved?', and 'Did we act in an ethically responsible way?'

Social pedagogic discourse

The discourse about what social pedagogy actually is was going on in several countries while this book was being written. Hegstrup (2007, p 54) thinks that this has to do with its 'lack of scientific "embededness" and thus lack of research documentation'. It seems that the social pedagogue needs a clearer theoretical base. However, we do not have time to wait for this. The social pedagogy practitioner does not have time to wait. The practitioner lives with a daily need for action. He meets his clients and is constantly intervening in their lives. He needs theory and tools, today, tomorrow and the whole of next week. That is the reason for this book. Even if we are unable to state clearly what social pedagogy is, we can look at what we *do* when we are engaged in our practice. This book is a summary of some of this practice. It is not all-encompassing. Writing an all-encompassing book about such practice would be an impossible project. However, I think I can safely say that it is comprehensive. It includes much of my own personal experience, linked to some of the most current theoretical discussions. One of the main aims of the book is to create something that approaches a link between theoretical social pedagogic discourses and what the social pedagogy practitioner actually does.[5] I have made the assumption that there is a need for such a book, as most authors of books about social pedagogy are not practice-oriented. According to Hegstrup (2007), the majority of those who write such books (in Denmark) are sociologists, and thus preoccupied with a particular angle of social pedagogy.

The chemistry teacher who was open to adopting a different understanding 'tomorrow' had an excellent attitude towards his subject. He established an understanding, and he adopted a perspective where he was willing to change if given access to knowledge providing a different view. That is how I would like this book to be understood. It describes my understanding of my subject. As such, the book is anchored in time – and, at the same time, open to criticism.

I hope that you will find it useful.

Notes

[1] In the main, I am using Norwegian and Nordic circumstances as my starting point, but without taking on the task of giving a comprehensive description of this starting point.

[2] In some parts of this book, I use other terms, for example, 'milieu therapist', 'adult' and 'helper'. This is mostly in order to vary the language. Even if this book is written by a teacher in the child welfare programme at a higher education institution, I have chosen not to use the designation child welfare worker. This is because I feel that the work that is being described is not unambiguously linked to one professional group. Social educators, preschool teachers, teachers, social workers, child and youth workers, and unskilled people may equally benefit from the book.

[3] I have chosen to talk about the social pedagogue as 'he'. I have made this choice because this is my own gender. Besides, it is more reader-friendly to use a single-gender term than the more cumbersome 'he/she'.

[4] I sometimes use other terms, for example, 'children' or 'young people' and 'those needing help'. This is necessary in order to vary the language.

[5] In parallel with my writing of this book, Roger Mathiesen is working on a book about social pedagogy that leans more towards the theoretical aspect – with a particular focus on the pedagogical foundation of social pedagogy. We have to some extent cooperated along the way, and I presume that his presentation will complement my own practice-oriented perspective (see Mathiesen, 2008).

CHAPTER TWO

Theoretical perspectives on social pedagogy

In this chapter, I will investigate the concept of *social pedagogy*. Many people find it difficult to get a clear picture of what it actually is, probably largely because we are trying to understand a complex field of practice. Gjertsen (2010, p 59) does not mince his words when he says that 'the theoretical understanding of social pedagogy is unclear'. He points to the fact that social pedagogy has had different traditions in different countries, and, as a consequence, is understood differently in different practice fields. At the same time, we have to take into account the fact that social pedagogy finds itself in a particular historical situation. Eriksson (2005) suggests that we regard the current situation as a formative phase. She writes that such a phase is hallmarked by the need to legitimise, define and demonstrate the practice of social pedagogy, and to indicate and define its boundaries with other fields. She points out that social pedagogy has become an academic field in recent years. In the longer term, it is feasible that this may come to define it more clearly, but that it will be more difficult to define its content in the short term. Academisation implies increased reflection upon its practices, and, therefore, a phase of increased uncertainty.

At the same time, there is a danger in mystifying what is complex. I want to emphasise my belief that it really *is* possible to discover something about the topic of this book, but only if we examine it extremely thoroughly. It can only be understood through an investigative attitude. That is what I am attempting to achieve.

One way to investigate a concept is to look up what the actual word, or the term, means. With a compound word, it is often easier to discover things by dividing it into its two constituent parts. Some might think this a little laborious, but we sometimes take concepts for granted and, therefore, fail to spend enough time trying to understand them. Investigating the concepts we use is an important part of our professional competence. In our case, dividing the word in this way shows us that we are talking about a 'social' pedagogy – you might say a socially oriented pedagogy. The first part of the concept tells us that we are dealing with something that has a social side, that is, something that happens between people. The second part tells us that this 'something' has to do with education, or upbringing.

Pedagogisk ordbok (Bø and Helle, 2002, p 235) gives us a useful short version, with four definitions of the concept. They are:

- various movements within pedagogic theory and practice dating from around 1900, emphasising the social and societal aims of upbringing;

- pedagogic theory and practice concerned with the effect of teaching and upbringing on the social development of pupils;[1]
- theory, methods and activity on the border between social and educational/ pedagogic/care work in society, that is, work (especially among children and young people) that is done socially and/or culturally with a consciously preventive, educational, habilitating or rehabilitating aim, and partly also with a treatment aim. Defined in this way, social pedagogic services in schools, *milieu* therapy and organised cultural and leisure activities, for example, youth clubs, outreach services and so on, are all covered by the term 'social pedagogy'; and
- an academic subject with varying content at university colleges and universities.

It is the content of the third definition that is closest to what this book is about. We have thus discovered that social pedagogy has clear references to pedagogy (as a more general concept) and to social work. Myhre (1982) writes that social pedagogy is the study of upbringing with an accompanying practice; and that social work is support work (Levin, 2004).

The simplest explanation of social pedagogy that I have come across is that it concerns the work carried out by child welfare pedagogues and social educators. But, of course, such an explanation is too simple. Is it, for example, the case that all work carried out by everybody with these job titles can always be called social pedagogy? Can we also talk about them practising social pedagogy if they are acting unethically, or if they only partly follow a recognised method within their practice field? And what if an untrained colleague is working alongside the social pedagogue, are the actions of this colleague not social pedagogic? Mathiesen (1999) mentions this explanation, and writes that it is what we might understand as something purely practical. Nevertheless, the explanation has some value. It puts us on the trail of a possible answer. It tells us something about the clients who are at the receiving end of the social pedagogue's work. These are mostly children, young people and their families, who, in some way or other, are living in a difficult or marginal situation. The social pedagogue has some form of help function in relation to these people.

> So, as we have seen, one aspect of social pedagogy concerns working with people. We could say that social pedagogy is practice.

The next trail can be found in books and other specialist literature written by social science-oriented researchers and technical authors, and in official reports about various social groups. These are often groups that for various reasons are not included in one or several sections of the extended social community. Reading this literature, we find perspectives on how to understand the mechanisms that expel people and groups, as well as suggestions of how to deal with them. However, these suggestions are rarely about individuals or small groups. In this context, social pedagogy often concentrates on larger groups and the forces in society that rule their lives.

> Another aspect of social pedagogy is more closely connected to research, hypotheses and politics. We could say that social pedagogy is theory.

So, we see that social pedagogy consists of both theory and practice. We could say that the theory sums up (good) practice, and subsequently gives guidance on practice; while practice itself is the tool, or the action part, of theory, where ideas are put into practice with the people concerned. In addition, practice gives material back to the theoretical level, so that the theories can be further developed. A field that comprises both theory and practice is obviously complex; dividing it in this way helps us to get the overall picture. However, most, if not all, practice fields are like this. What is it that is particularly characteristic of social pedagogy in this respect?

In social pedagogy, the relationship between theory and practice is arranged in a particular way. The most important reason for this is that social pedagogy has a very wide *subject field*. I will explain what I mean by the concept of 'subject' in this context: it refers to that which is *the subject of interest* in the field. In social pedagogy, both social and educational situations and questions on all levels from individuals via groups to society are subjects of interest to the social pedagogue. There was, for example, a hint of this in the conversation between Mette and Trond. It is this breadth that is a strength of the field, but also a problem. The breadth provides an opportunity for a diversity of angles when the social pedagogue carries out his investigations and assessments. However, it also makes social pedagogy difficult to grasp, and, therefore, difficult to handle. Madsen (2006, p 58) describes the subject field as 'individuals and groups who find themselves in conflicts zones in society, in the tension field between integration and marginalisation or actual expulsion'. At the same time, Madsen shows that his interest is more related to what he calls 'intervention … in conflict zones where the stability of a society is threatened' (Madsen, 2006, p 58). This points in the direction of a sociologically oriented social pedagogy.

My own interest is mainly directed towards individuals and small groups who find themselves in marginalised or potentially marginalised positions. The subject in this book is, therefore, not quite the same as in Madsen's case. When I emphasise individuals (and small groups, like families) as the subject, thoughts can easily stray into the field of psychology, but that is not where we are heading either. The distinct orientation towards the individual found in much of traditional psychology gives an approach that is different to that of social pedagogy. In other words, social pedagogy is neither sociology nor psychology. However, in the range that covers the areas of interest in these fields – between individual and society –we may discover a subject that is different.

In Denmark, the concept 'common third' has often been used as a term for the subject of social pedagogy. The thinking behind it is that the social pedagogue (one) and the client (another) in social pedagogic situations come together in a common third space, which they develop from their individual positions (Lihme,

1988; Madsen, 2006). Lihme writes that it is not the child or young person who is the subject, but what the social pedagogue creates together with the child or the young person. What they create together is something that the child or the young person needs in their life in order to be included in the community. Sociology and psychology are professions closely related to social pedagogy, but, as we have seen, they are not the same. Maybe we could say that by using perspectives from both, social pedagogy builds a bridge between them. Professionals who view knowledge as spanning a wide field often find it natural to use the concept 'holistic'. Bronfenbrenner (1979) has created a holistic perspective on human development that directs its gaze at all levels, from micro to macro. His particular contribution was to connect events from different levels. It is true that he was a psychologist by profession, but his overall interest can easily be regarded as parallel to the interest of social pedagogy.

A practice field without a clearly defined knowledge base is in danger of being misunderstood. It is not easy to state with complete clarity which perspective or perspectives together form social pedagogic theory and, thus, describe social pedagogic practice. Therefore, everybody who claims to work with social pedagogy in one context or another may be able to claim the ability to say something significant about what it actually is. In other fields of practice, the subject is narrower and more clearly defined. Let us, for example, take a look at general pedagogy. We find it clearly relates to teaching. It has a better defined practice and a better defined theoretical understanding. General pedagogic theories are, therefore, easier to grasp; there are fewer arenas for general pedagogic practice, and the methodical measures are easier to describe.

The broad subject field is not just about the practitioner (who will often be preoccupied with everyday dilemmas and perhaps individual children) and the theorist (who is interested in more general perspectives) not using the same concepts. Many regard social and educational work with people as different from theoretical analyses of forces in society on a macro level. Implied in this is that different social pedagogues could draw the conclusion that they do not share the same type of subject, the same professional interest. This presents us with the slightly odd situation that social pedagogic theory in some situations can seem disconnected from social pedagogic practice. Maybe Mathiesen (1999) is right when he suggests that social pedagogic practitioners are not that bothered by the seemingly blurred and composite theories in the field. Maybe they are more preoccupied by the profession's lack of status than its lack of theoretical clarity. On the other hand, we could say that being preoccupied with something implies precisely the process of abstraction. So, the practitioner is faced with the duality of, on the one hand, having to act and, on the other, not getting away from abstraction about his practice.

Instead of asking what social pedagogy is, we could ask what characterises the *skilful practice of social pedagogy*. Madsen (2006) does this, and I will be taking a look at his answer to the question. He divides the answer into three parts, claiming that the science of social pedagogy is theory, methods and values. The theory represents a multidisciplinary knowledge base that we have to expect the social pedagogue practitioner to be familiar with and to put into use. The methods are *what social pedagogues actually do*. They are not simply the application of techniques, but are always connected to what the client needs. The values of social pedagogic practice are 'the dimension of formal or informal criteria for how the knowledge shall be applied, and to what end' (Madsen, 2006, p 50). We are talking about the ethics of social pedagogy. Based on this, we can say that social pedagogy rests on three pillars: theory, practice and values. There is a reciprocal relationship between them: they are interdependent and interconnected. We can say that they are mutually dependent on each other.

When the social pedagogy practitioner practises his profession, he is at once doing something ordinary and something specific. Ordinary because everyday situations are his arena, and there is an ordinary side to being with clients (Grønvold, 1997). The social pedagogue eats with his clients, helps them with their homework, goes for walks and watches TV with them, and innumerable other ordinary things. His pedagogic work takes place in these ordinary, everyday social situations. There are, of course, also situations with a more technical and educational orientation, for example, when the social pedagogue arranges a specific conversation with the young person. But even these conversations manifest everyday social exchanges. Because these situations often are very ordinary, it is not always easy, for example, to explain what distinguishes social pedagogic exchanges and interventions in an institution from the exchanges that ordinarily take place in a family.

The specific practice of the social pedagogy practitioner is one that emerges from theory. In addition, his work is founded on ethical guidelines, and it is more systematic than 'the ordinary and everyday'. The systematic element is disclosed by the social pedagogue planning his interventions and having an understanding of the relevant theory applied. He then evaluates his interventions to discover the effect they had, as well as his use of theory. Based on this, we can say that the practice-oriented social pedagogue does not use theory any less than his theoretically oriented colleague. Trond uses theory just as much as Mette does. The main difference is that they do not use theory on the same abstraction level, and that the practitioner uses his reflection on theory in order to achieve a well-founded base for intervention with his clients.

In a textbook like this, it is useful to have a definition of its main topic. Personally, I have not wanted to define the actual concept of social pedagogy because it is so multifaceted and, to some extent, sprawling. On the other hand, having decided to limit my writing to the social pedagogue practitioner and his work, it is my duty to give a more precise definition of this, the practising, element. By choice, I have not written a concise and unambiguous definition. The problem with such definitions is that they are almost incomprehensible, because you try to include as much concrete information as possible in as few words as possible. Instead, I have written what I call a defining description.

Practising social pedagogy can be understood as a collective term for pedagogically oriented practices based on a professional assessment and carried out in ordinary, everyday situations. These are directed towards children and young people who need help, or to situations where the need for help can be prevented, and towards their families, networks and immediate environment. The main aim of the work is inclusion in a community. Interventions are guided by values and theory.

The three main elements – intervention, values and theory – are given separate descriptions below:

- Practical engagement takes the form of diverse *interventions* aimed at including clients in social communities and helping them to solve problems, particularly through increasing their own problem-solving competence. The social pedagogy practitioner works with both individuals and groups in a holistic perspective. The most common arenas for this change-oriented activity are ordinary, everyday situations, or situations that resemble the ordinary and everyday. The interventions are, therefore, ordinary in the sense that they are directed towards ordinary human (social) engagement. They differ from other human engagement by also being characterised by systematic assessments with a theoretical foundation.
- Social pedagogic practices are guided by *values* that are formulated in ethical guidelines and ethical reflection on actions. Some of the most important values-oriented guidelines in social pedagogy are that it is subject- and resource-oriented. The practice is also founded on the idea of inclusion and equality across ethnic and cultural differences.
- Social pedagogic practice is grounded in several theoretical perspectives. One of these is social pedagogic *theory*, which ensures a focus on processes in society to do with inclusion, exclusion and marginality. To the extent that this theory focuses on the individual, it is the individual as a participant in a group and a community. There is also a focus on the individual in his own right, but not without including the context in which he lives. The practising element is also guided by theory from other professional fields, which are brought in as part-perspectives. Here, we are talking about sociological and psychological theory and theories of learning and socialising, communication, and group processes. These theoretical links bring science into the everyday situations where the social pedagogy practitioner operates.

The three elements in this description deal with different aspects of the phenomenon. They are practice, values and theory, as also described by Madsen (2006). I will look more closely at these later in this chapter. The positioning of two other professional perspectives in the description is also important: these are psychology and sociology.

Before I continue, I would like to emphasise my suggestion that ethnicity is also a factor in the inclusion ideal in social pedagogic practice. A client's need for help is not necessarily only related to the fact that he has a difficult life. There can be many reasons for his marginalisation, or the danger of marginalisation. One reason may be that he belongs to an minority ethnic group.[2] Hamburger (2001) claims that culture is a plausible explanation for the marginalisation of people. He writes that a person's cultural origins may be interpreted and constructed both into and out of situations. He shows that in situations where there is an easy flow of communication, participants can be observed focusing on similarities and common experience. In other situations, which for various reasons are more conflictual and where communication is more difficult, cultural differences are often constructed as a reason for exclusion. Such communication patterns are often not obvious to participants.

Social pedagogic theory

This book puts the spotlight on social pedagogic practice, and, consequently, most of the chapters deal with practice. However, in *this* chapter, I will take a closer look at social pedagogy as theory. The account that follows is not complete, but it attempts to give a brief picture of what we understand by this concept. For the most part, my literary references are from Scandinavia. Those who want to go further and look at social pedagogy in other countries will find references in, for example, Madsen (2006) and Mathiesen (1999, 2008).

Let us go back in time a little in order to grasp the historical foundation for social pedagogy. Both Madsen (2005) and Eriksson and Markström (2000) describe the past 400–500 years as a time of great upheaval in European society. With the passing of the Middle Ages and its feudal society and the emergence of the age of exploration, modern science and the capitalist economy, relations between people also changed. The emergence of an industrial society led to the disappearance of old structures and, thus, an increasing need for upbringing to be founded on the logic of this new society. Because large numbers of people gradually became wage-earners, they had to face demands for different understanding and behaviour. According to Eriksson and Markström (2000), the ideas of the French Revolution about a person's right to independence and formation were significant for the development of social pedagogic thought. The society that emerged at this time also meant that citizens developed new competencies. Industrial society demanded, for example, that the workers kept certain hours. New processes of integration and marginalisation developed. Those who were included found their place in this new economy and adjusted to the new set of norms. But not everyone became integrated. Madsen thinks that society's attempt to integrate everybody forms the basis of what we today call social pedagogy. He writes that social pedagogy can be understood as society's way to relate to those who deviate from the norm (Madsen, 2005). He also gives an account of how integration work is carried out in various ways in different historical periods. The 18th and 19th centuries saw the emergence of a strong tradition of exclusion and confinement. According to Madsen, this particular way of solving the problem has grown ever-more advanced, even up to our own time. Today, however, the dismantling of institutions and the prevention of problems are far more important strategies for those who cannot find their place in society.

The integrated and the marginalised are mostly not defined in the same way today as they were in the old industrial society. Social pedagogic practice functions in societal and time-limited contexts. It is therefore vital that social pedagogy must understand the society and the period it operates in. Frønes (2001) understands being marginalised in our society as something other than not having a job. Today, the marginalised person is someone who does not realise his potential, who is unable to find a 'suitable' identity in modern society. In this context, shame is more closely connected to one's own life story than whether one contributes to society by paying tax. In other words, what is shameful is not having an effective life story (Frønes, 2001; Storø, 2005). At the same time, it is true that those in work are included because they have access to financial capital. Money is definitely a means of 'buying into' many of the facets of modern society. These days, getting an education is also generally regarded as a useful inclusion strategy for individuals. Madsen (2006) says that it is important to focus on the fact that society – here understood as those who are included – is constantly developing new ways of distinguishing between those who are included and those who are marginalised. Put differently, we could say that the definition of what is normal is changeable. It is those who define themselves as *normal* who define others as *outsiders*. The distinction between inside and outside is usually based on morality, that is, the civic morality that prevails at any one time. One important aspect of such distinctions is the discussion about what Madsen (2006, p 17) calls 'self guilt'. The question of whether marginalisation can be blamed on society or on the marginalised themselves is important. There is a significant difference between defining the marginalised as useless, maladjusted and lazy, or as vulnerable and unlucky. It is, of course, also possible to use more positive concepts to define those who are marginalised. You could, for example, talk about alternative lifestyles, or of people who 'chose a different scale of values to the traditional one'. Some people find their identity in a marginal position (Storø, 2001). The social pedagogic concept of marginalisation is usually understood as 'a relationship between people and society, not as a human characteristic' (Hämäläinen, 2005, p 35). That enables *working with* individual marginalisation processes.

According to Madsen (2006, p 19), social pedagogy addresses three different factors: 'the approach to the individual; his social and cultural conditions; and the complex interplay between people and their social environment'. He further states that 'it is the task of social pedagogy to create conditions for social participation in mainstream communities' (Madsen 2006, p 19). This can be understood on both an individual and a societal level. The social pedagogue practitioner works in many, quite different, situations, and is therefore faced with relatively different challenges that can be linked by these formulations. As far as social pedagogic practice is concerned, Madsen (2006, p 19) writes that it 'seeks to create and re-create binding and mutual social situations between individuals and communities in society's conflict zones'. The term 'conflict zones' refers to the conflict between the included and the marginalised, and the definition processes I have already mentioned.

Another author who writes about social pedagogic theory is Roger Mathiesen. He refers to Paul Natorp (1854–1924), who is regarded by many as the pioneering writer on social pedagogy. According to Mathiesen (1999), Natorp argued that social pedagogy is a *practical philosophy* about the upbringing and social education that enables inclusion in the community. He described social pedagogy as *the pedagogy of the will*. Mathiesen (1999, p 87) writes that:

> Natorp's focus on the human will implies an understanding that people can choose how they relate to each other. But by focusing on the influence of the community in this context, he states that choices made by individuals are influenced by relational and social conditions.

Mathiesen (1999, p 59) also writes that a person's ability to think rationally and reflect on his actions indicates that he is 'responsible for his actions, and that a person therefore is the subject in his own life'. We can see that this clearly indicates a positive view of human beings, with a focus on people's potential both as individuals and social beings. Mathiesen (1999, p 15) also comments on Natorp's assertion that 'Man can only become man through human interaction', adding that this 'implies having to think in a socially responsible way'. In other words, the social pedagogy practitioner cannot solely focus on the individual client. He must also bear in mind the client's situation, both in the local environment and in a broader perspective. Natorp adds that 'the goal of upbringing is the socialisation and moral development of one's whole life' (Mathiesen, 1999, p 55). We see from this that the upbringing provided by the social pedagogue not only concerns giving individual children a reasonable life. The child also needs to be brought up and educated to become a social individual. At the same time, Natorp is thinking about the child themself, and (as recounted by Mathiesen) maintains that 'any enrichment of individualism is an enrichment of the community, and a genuine community will be able to provide space for individualism' (Mathiesen, 1999, p 55). Eriksson and Markström (2000) emphasise Natorp's idea that human beings and the community are dependent on each other, and that the community liberates rather than limits people. The Norwegian pedagogue Tone Sævi (2007, p 130, emphasis in original) states something similar by claiming that:

> in the lives of adults and children, pedagogy is meaningful as a personal, immediate, diverse, reciprocal *togetherness*, which lasts for moments, but paradoxically also has an enduring quality; and its most profound goal is the contribution to making the child *human*.

This brings us to the concept of formation, which is regarded as a very important concept in social pedagogy (Madsen, 2006; Mathiesen, 1999, 2008). It is precisely in the concept of formation that we find a clarification of social pedagogy, seen in relation to the general concept of pedagogy. Formation is a difficult concept. It is easier to imagine that we learn something than that we are formed to or into something. The concept alludes to a handing down of norms and values by society and the parent generation, and as such represents something that is conserved (Savater, 1998). However, according to Savater (1998, p 133), in this process, we also demonstrate 'the desirable or frightening possibilities which exist, but have yet to become reality'. In other words, formation is also an invitation. When the growing generation learns about the culture and the presumptions that their parents built their lives on, it is provided with tools to create something new, something different and overriding. It is this dynamic concept of formation that is most useful in the theoretical landscape of this book. Formation means to absorb *what is* and to acquire tools to discover *what could be*.

Bisgaard (2006) points to what he calls three classic pedagogic aspects: knowledge, skills and attitudes. At the same time, he shows that classic pedagogy has particularly stressed the first one of these. Because social pedagogic practice must be regarded as a pedagogy that is chiefly practised outside the classroom, as I have described it in this book, the last two aspects are obviously especially important. However, the knowledge aspect is also important to the social pedagogue, as in providing knowledge that the client can use in his everyday life. You could call this aspect *knowledge about the ordinary (and everyday)*.

Bisgaard (2006, p 9) defines formation:

> partly as a process: to form (as in developing or maturing) or to be formed (as a result of influence from other people or environments), and partly as a product or result which is the outcome of such a process. Understood in this way, the concept of formation in a pedagogic sense often coincides with concepts like upbringing and education.

For a large part, the social pedagogic practice described in this book is connected to the aspect of upbringing and social education. The most important reason for this is probably that child welfare pedagogues and other professional practitioners working in corresponding parts of the practice field find themselves in positions where they are responsible for the upbringing of children and young people. Sometimes, they work 'in place of a parent', for example, when the child has been taken into care. Other times, they contribute to a child's upbringing alongside the parents. In this context, upbringing can be understood in diverse ways: first, as the bringing up of individual children or young people to become members of their immediate social community – be it the family, foster family or institution – as well as at school; and, second, as contributing towards the transfer and stimulation of knowledge, skills and attitudes that will increase the children's or young people's opportunities for inclusion in society. In this sense, the socialised child will be the child who is included. Pedagogy does not have a clear view on the question of adjustment versus change (cf. Eriksson and Markström, 2000). Here, we find an important dilemma, which can be formulated in the question of whether formation as a pedagogic phenomenon solely implies adjustment to the norms of society, or whether it is characterised by a change process. Put in a different way: do the ideas and practices of pedagogy contribute to conformity or liberation? I will return to this question a little later in this chapter.

Both Madsen and Mathiesen write about *pedagogic emergencies*. Madsen (2006) talks about this as one of two development tracks in Danish social pedagogy,[3] while Mathiesen (1999, p 12) understands such situations as the real *theme and task of social pedagogy*. The notion of pedagogic emergencies is close to Eriksson and Markström's (2000) notion of *vulnerable life situations*. These are situations that require 'activity which attempts to compensate for deficiencies or faults in the upbringing of the growing generation' (Mathiesen, 1999, p 12). This understanding implies that the task of the social pedagogue practitioner is to step in where something has gone wrong with the conditions under which children and young people are growing up. The problem may be in the family, but it may also have its roots in the community where the children, young people and their families live. It is important to note this point in social pedagogic theory. The notion of an emergency situation indicates that something has gone wrong and needs to be rectified. When we talk about upbringing in a social pedagogic context, what we often really mean is 're-upbringing'. In other words, a pedagogy that tries to correct problems that have occurred during the child or young person's upbringing in childhood and adolescence, and in particular life conditions. It is important to regard all these conditions as a whole. It is not just the case that the social pedagogue should come in as 'a better educator than the child's parents'. He also needs to have a sharp focus on the more general life conditions under which the child grew up and was brought up. Such a focus should help the social pedagogue practitioner to understand the reasons for the problem in the first place, and thus to avoid apportioning blame for the situation he is working with. The notion of re-upbringing will, therefore, often mean enabling parents to correct their own mistakes, rather than transferring the task to professionals (ie the social pedagogue). Some situations will nevertheless occur when the professionals have to step in and assume full responsibility for children and young people. Here, I am particularly thinking of situations where they are taken into care by the child welfare services, and subjected to a care order. Another important point is that the social pedagogue who has the competence to help solve pedagogic emergency situations also ought to be able to contribute to the prevention of such situations. It is commonly assumed that the social pedagogic practice field should have tools for preventive work, for counteracting marginalisation processes and lessening their effect.

Social pedagogy also has other roots. Eriksson and Markström (2000) mention two in particular. One is the US tradition of social work represented by Jane Addams and Mary Richmond. The other is parts of 20th-century pedagogic literature. The American John Dewey and the Brazilian Paulo Freire are particularly important in this connection. Gjertsen (2010) also shows us the parallel development of social work and social pedagogy over the past hundred years. At the same time, he explains how social pedagogy has its origins in fundamental discussions about pedagogy (see also Levin, 2004; Mathiesen, 2008). Eriksson (2005) also points to the proximity of social pedagogy and the theoretical tradition in psychology. These may have had a closer relationship in Norway than in the other Nordic countries. In Norway, milieu therapy has also been coupled with social pedagogy in the training of child welfare pedagogues (Grønvold, 2000).

The fundamental issues of social pedagogy lead us to its more practice-oriented dimension. Gjertsen (2010) explains it by saying that some people understand social pedagogy as one of two traditions within social work (the other is social casework). He refers to the definition of social work given by the International Federation of Social Workers (IFSW), where values like 'principles of human rights and social justice' and 'empowerment and liberation of people to enhance their well-being' (recounted in Gjertsen, 2010, p 47) are benchmarks. Gjertsen (2010, p 47) summarises the ethical principles as 'humanitarian and democratic ideals, with its values based on respect for the equality, worth and dignity of all people'. A parallel to this way of thinking can be found in Eriksson and Markström (2000, p 74, emphasis in original), who write that 'the social pedagogic task has become to *support, stimulate and mobilise* people'. In this, we can see clear parallels to Freire (1990), who was particularly interested in the opportunities pedagogy offers for liberation.

This superior level of social pedagogic theory, where, in particular, Madsen (2005, 2006) operates, is first and foremost useful as a theory of explanation or of understanding. Such theories tell us something about phenomena like marginalisation, poverty and crime – why they occur and which functions they have in different contexts (Eriksson and Markström, 2000). Gjertsen (2010, p 65) touches on this when he writes that the theoretical foundation is important 'in order to understand how psychological, social and material conditions result in social and pedagogic emergencies'. This is very important, and shows, among other things, what distinguishes social pedagogy from, for example, the more individually based explanation models in psychology. But is this theory just as useful as *action theory*? Using the concept 'action theory', I intend to direct attention towards the theoretical reasoning for the kind of intervention the social pedagogue practitioner ought to initiate in the emergency situations that he works in. There is a parallel to this in Parton and O'Byrne (2000), who describe a failure to articulate and develop concepts and theories *for* practice in social work.[4] They write that new regulations about being user-oriented, working towards empowering the clients and promoting their independence do not give clear guidelines for action or an understanding of the skills, knowledge and theory needed by the practitioners. The focus here is on its usefulness in practice.

The relationship between explanation theory and action theory in social pedagogy may be one of the reasons why it is regarded as difficult, and why there is disagreement about what social pedagogy really is. My impression is that social pedagogic theory on the whole has developed as a superior theory of explanation. The writers who have dealt with this topic have to a far lesser extent been engaged in developing an action theory that social pedagogue practitioners can use in their daily work. The theory is often found on a group and societal level, while the practising social pedagogue's work is with individuals. All theory can, of course, be potential action theory, but, as we saw in the conversation between Trond and Mette at the start of this book, the practitioner might regard theory operating on a high level as pretty much removed from the practical reality where he encounters his clients. It is my view that this situation can be called a crisis between theory and practice in social pedagogy. Even if social pedagogy in many respects is a practically oriented profession, it seems that practice is not sufficiently present in the profession's theoretical foundation.

Mathiesen also touches on what we could call social pedagogic competence. He thinks that it:

> implies focusing on the relational conditions under which the child was brought up, in order to discover what went wrong with the content and the structure. The goal becomes finding out which relational conditions are required in order for the child to be given the care that was missing. (Mathiesen, 1999, p 57)

Here, we see that the focus is on the outcomes of the pedagogic emergency situations. The task of the social pedagogue is to give the child something they have never had.

Social constructionism

Having presented a few fundamental assumptions of social pedagogic theory, I now need to expand on my own perspective on this theory. I have already hinted at it earlier in the book, but will now clarify it further. One of my goals with this book is to write about a social pedagogy that is oriented towards the practical. Another is to investigate whether social constructionist theory can expand fundamental thinking about social pedagogy. It is the second of these goals that I will deal with in this section. Many authors have attempted to clarify what Eriksson and Markström (2000) mean by what they call the core of social pedagogy. The conclusion is usually that it is difficult to give an unambiguous answer to the question. Could it be that it is the wrong question? A question formulated as 'What is …', which seeks to define the essence of something, could be criticised for seeking a fundamental truth about a phenomenon that can hardly be described as something final. Another way to pose the question might be to ask what social pedagogy is *not*. The focus would then be moved away from the essence, and, instead, boundaries would be established: boundaries against other fields. This may be important enough, and I hint at such boundaries in this book. However, drawing boundaries does not contribute much to the understanding of what is located *within* the boundaries.

A third way to ask the question might be: 'What *could* social pedagogy be?' Such a question would open up the possibility of social pedagogy changing dynamically in line with changes in society, as emphasised by, among others, Hämäläinen (2005) and Eriksson and Markström (2000). In particular, it is the understanding of what constitutes a problem, and what should be done about it, that is changing (Madsen, 2006). Social pedagogy, therefore, needs to be oriented towards such change processes. The question of what it *could* be is a question oriented towards development, while the other two questions are more static.

This gives us the opportunity to look at social constructionist theory as an important theory in social pedagogy. In this account, I am leaning towards, among others, the British writer Vivien Burr, who uses the psychological practice field as her starting point. This is interesting because, according to Burr (2003) herself, a social constructionist perspective is in many ways incompatible with traditional psychology. She says that the term is used almost exclusively by writers in the field of psychology. Nevertheless, she makes it quite clear that social constructionism is multidisciplinary, that is, it encompasses a range of different approaches within the social sciences. In particular, Burr mentions sociology as a relevant field, because of a parallel interest in some of the same phenomena. This is exactly where we find social pedagogy, in the intersecting point between psychology and sociology. But I see no reason to stop at that. In the spirit of constructionism, I want to try to show that this multidisciplinary perspective is parallel to what is the case with social pedagogy. My hypothesis, therefore, is that it ought to be *particularly* linked to social pedagogic theory.

Burr is reluctant to give a brief definition of social constructionism. However, she mentions a few important basic assumptions within this perspective. First of all, the perspective implies not taking any knowledge for granted. In social constructionism, reality is not perceived as final or objective. Instead, this view gives us the opportunity to regard the phenomena we perceive as reality in many different ways. As such, social constructionism is in sharp contrast to a positivist view of reality and science, where the most important basic assumption is that there is an objectively defined reality. The next assumption is that our understanding of reality is connected to the specific historical and cultural context we find ourselves in. These first two assumptions give us a clear reminder that what we perceive as real may be perceived differently by other people, in other contexts, at other times and in other cultures. In other words, this view means that knowledge must be regarded as a subjective, context-bound dimension, that is, as a temporary understanding of reality. The third assumption is that we do not define knowledge about reality as individuals, but as participants in social processes. Acting together, we construct understandings that are useful to us in order to understand ourselves and our surroundings. A lot of this occurs through the social processes connected to language. In this way, our understandings become more than subjective, individual understandings. They become intersubjective understandings. This means that understandings are shared between several subjects who act together and who have conversations with each other. When some understandings have greater validity and a longer lifespan than others, we think of them as expressions of a culture. Burr (2003, p 5) talks about 'negotiated' understandings, and, as her fourth assumption, points to different understandings inviting different kinds of action.

Note that I write about understandings in the plural. In a social constructionist perspective, we can imagine everybody constructing and 'carrying with them' several understandings of what appears to be the same phenomenon at the same time. Within each individual, there is also an ongoing negotiation about what ought to be the dominating understandings, and what kind of linguistic expression they should be given. According to Burr (2003), this is where a pure social constructionist perspective in psychology runs into problems, because it does not take the individual and individual differences into account. She is advocating, therefore, a social constructionism that also includes a look at individual feelings. Only by doing that will we get an understanding of why people sometimes act contrary to what must be presumed to be in their own best interest.

I have chosen to understand Burr's assumptions on a fairly concrete level. Through linguistic interaction, we can let wonder and reflection create new ways of seeing ourselves and others. This, in turn, creates new ways of acting.

This whole range of assumptions (which, in itself, is a social construction) is one of the results of many attempts to capture a view of knowledge for the social sciences that is distinct from that of the natural sciences. Social pedagogy is inextricably linked to social science and to the hermeneutic knowledge tradition. It is, therefore, reasonable to make this juxtaposition of social pedagogy and social constructionism. I am emphasising the close connection between these two perspectives because I would like to look at what social constructionism can give to social pedagogy. For me, two especially important areas stand out.

First, by revitalising the pedagogical element, social constructionism contributes to a better understanding of the complexity of social pedagogy. Traditionally, pedagogy has been strongly bound to the classroom. In everyday conversations, the concept is often understood in connection with schooling, and with teacher and pupil standpoints. Such a view has a strongly hierarchical understanding: the teacher as the supplier of knowledge and the pupil as the recipient. Social pedagogy has a different view on learning, as per my previous argument with reference to Bisgaard (2006). It perceives pedagogy as something beyond pure learning.

When the term social pedagogy is used in schools, greater emphasis is placed, for example, on 'theory, methods and activity in the borderland between social and pedagogic work in society' (Bø and Helle, 2002, p 235). The aim of such measures may be both 'protecting the physical and mental health of pupils, increasing well-being and strengthening a sense of community' (Bø and Helle, 2002, p 236), and creating a basis for understanding of process learning and group work that values pupil contributions. The social constructionist view is that knowledge is defined in social processes; not only the kind of knowledge that pedagogy traditionally has dealt with, but all knowledge. So, in this perspective, all knowledge, and, thus, all understanding, is socially constructed.

If we presuppose that understanding is negotiated socially: first, it is not possible to avoid the complex understanding of process that is necessary for these professional perspectives; and, second, the potential rigidity of traditional pedagogy may be exchanged for a much more dynamic openness to contributions other than the teacher's. We see that social constructionism puts the focus on people's own perceptions of what is real and what is right and wrong, good and bad, and so on. In this perspective, each and every one of us creates our own perceptions, and we can make the connection to the liberating functions that pedagogy can give to people. At the same time, we are not focusing on the individual as standing alone, but on individuals acting together. In other words, the constructions each and every one of us makes, we make as participants in social processes. This is where the social pedagogue practitioner is given the opportunity to act in ways different from the traditionally oriented pedagogue. A pedagogy that perceives the pedagogue as one of several potentially interacting people in a social construction process is qualitatively different from traditional pedagogy. In a social constructionist perspective, the social pedagogue has very few ready-made answers to offer his clients. Put in a different way, he does not have a curriculum to teach. However, he knows a lot about process, and he can give good advice about various ways to construct understandings so that the aims of inclusion and integration can be reached for those who are part of the process. The social pedagogue can also influence construction processes. This is the essence of the social pedagogue's work with clients. Connecting social pedagogy and social constructionism in this way, we see that social constructionism also gains something from this, namely, that constructions can have both a social and a pedagogic aim. This is important, as a lot of social constructionist literature has its origin in psychology. Social pedagogy, therefore, must create its own understanding of social constructionism.

Let us go back to Parton and O'Byrne (2000), who also suggest that constructionist social work puts the emphasis on process and on the opportunity that clients are given by the professionals to retell their story in a different way. According to this way of thinking, the professional's function is that he is an expert on process, while the client is said to have expertise about his or her own life. This is in parallel to what Durrant (1993) suggests as a working model for staff in institutions. We see that Parton and O'Byrne operate with two different types of knowledge and two different tasks that the professional and the client can contribute to, each from their own position. They further claim that this knowledge and these tasks must work together in relational meetings. For these authors, it is 'face-to-face work with clients' that makes practice what it is (Parton and O'Byrne, 2000, p 3). They further claim that all aspects of the understandings that can be identified in the meetings with clients are expressions of constructions. It is not obvious, for example, what may be called a problem, or what would constitute a solution. Such constructions must also be negotiated.

A social constructionist way of thinking thus offers those who are marginalised opportunities for new ways of constructing understandings, and, hence, obtaining new ways of acting that pave the way to participation in inclusion processes in the community. Berglund (2004, p 136) also makes a connection between the two perspectives: social pedagogy and social constructionism. He writes that he strongly believes in:

> a social work with both social and pedagogic elements. A social pedagogy which takes a narrative, salutogenetic approach and which is based on social constructionist theoretical reasoning. This implies that the social work becomes more of a pedagogic challenge than social engineering. The pedagogic starts from where the client is, uses ordinary, everyday social interaction as a resource and a source of energy, and is supported by what actually works. This puts the emphasis on opportunities and the capacity to change, rather than being fixated on the problem.[5]

What Berglund is proposing here is a division of labour between social pedagogic practice and social constructionist theory. He talks about 'a way to behave', in other words, the practical element that arises from concepts like 'narrative' and 'salutogenesis'. These are the active actions of the social pedagogue practitioner. He also talks about a social constructionist-oriented theory. It is in the interplay between this practical level and social pedagogic theory that Berglund sees good opportunities for working with children and young people.

The other area where social constructionism is a help to social pedagogy is by taking this pedagogy with it into a new era, namely, the postmodern society. According to Holst (2005, p 17), it is true that:

> The processes of individualisation and globalisation in modern society are a challenge to pedagogy and calls for fresh deliberation and analysis of the development and integrative capacity of communities, as well as an assessment of the relationship between the individual and the community in post-modern society.

With fresh ways of thinking about development processes and the relationship between the individual and community comes the need to think about pedagogic practices in a new way. We can no longer use a mechanical understanding of the relationship between teacher and pupil, between helper and those needing help, or between the marginalised person and society. An increased focus on the individual's self-construction also means that the client must be given the resources demanded by such constructions. Marginalised people's relationship with society can therefore now be understood in a different way. It can be seen in the light of shared constructions about what includes and what marginalises, how such processes actually happen, and, not least, how the person who is marginalised or in danger of becoming marginalised constructs his understandings. A linguistic example of this is when people who have experienced incest argue in favour of changing the term that is sometimes used about them as a group from 'incest victims' to 'those at risk of incest'. This is a clear example of a construction that points to a place away from victimhood.

I am not going to delve into thorough definitions of postmodernism in this book. I just want to mention that the concept, which has its origins in the 1930s, was meant to describe a way of thinking that represented something other than modernity's emphasis on objectivity and rationality (Parton and O'Byrne, 2000). Postmodern thinking is about the dissolution of 'accepted truth' and a focus on diversity and fragmentation. I shall briefly refer to Berglund (2004), who claims that what probably best characterises the postmodern is the understanding that we are constantly constructing the individual identity. We can see that this perspective is very closely related to social constructionist theory, which can be understood as a 'child of postmodernism'. Berglund gives us some important thoughts about social pedagogy in postmodernity. He writes about the understandings of reality we have developed in light of these new ways of thinking. In this connection, he sees the pedagogic project as 'getting to grips with and mastering a problematic childhood and difficult life conditions' (Berglund, 2004, p 135). He refers to the fact that studies of human problems in social work are nearly always retrospective and problem-focused. There is a risk of losing something essential in a person's constructive activity, because we live our lives forwards, not backwards.[6] Berglund (2004, p 137) goes on to write that 'people sometimes solve impossible life situations in unpredictable ways and seek positive routes to a solution which come as a surprise to the professionals'. He is interested in what actually happens in such processes. They are often difficult to map, and hard to explain scientifically. When we claim to be interested in individuals' constructions, it follows that we also have to acknowledge each individual 'recovery process' – that which creates meaning for each person. This may be close to Burr's (2003) presentation of social constructionism, which can be understood as a way of thinking in postmodernity. Incidentally, Parton and O'Byrne (2000) want to distinguish between the concepts 'social constructionism' and 'postmodernism'. They understand the first of these as a defined methodological understanding, while the second is understood as a more fundamental concept.

As social pedagogy focuses on the client in relation to society, it is vital to understand constructions in light of the society where they are being used at any one time. In this context, 'society' can be understood in both a narrow and a broad sense, that is, both as the social group that constitutes the individual's closest circle, and also as society as a whole. Such a view gives social interaction greater significance than we have previously been used to (Berglund, 2004). We are not only interacting with other people; we are constructing ourselves as a part of the social process. Current postmodern logic therefore appears to be a useful perspective on social pedagogy. At first glance, this is contrary to the claims of several authors: namely, that social pedagogy is inextricably linked to problems of marginalisation in industrial society (Holst, 2005; Madsen, 2005).[7] I still maintain that the fundamental issues in social pedagogy, which are linked to whether individuals and groups are on the *inside* or on the *outside*, are relevant in both industrial and postmodern societies. On the other hand, it is important to try to construct understandings that spring from the context in which one finds oneself. In postmodern times, therefore, marginalisation looks different to what it did in industrial society. As previously mentioned, Frønes (2001) and others write that where it was previously considered shameful not to have a job, in our time, shame is more linked to how you present yourself. So, according to this way of thinking, if you can present yourself as a self-realising individual who has a meaningful existence, you avoid being part of something shameful. You avoid being marginal.

We can see that, in many ways, modern social pedagogy is dependent on a social constructionist perspective. *Inside* and *outside* are not finite categories; they are social constructions. Gustavsson (2008, p 10) points out that, in our time, the social pedagogic interest is not only directed towards 'what distinguishes the so-called "normal" from "the abnormal"', but rather towards how normality/deviation and participation/exclusion are constructed in society's complex socialisation processes'. In other words, the constructions are continuous social processes.

Linking social pedagogy's focus on pedagogic emergency situations to social constructionism might at first sight seem like something of a paradox. The unsuccessful, or in other ways problematic, upbringing that the social pedagogue's clients have been exposed to surely makes it the professional's duty to repair damage, deal with the traumatic and prevent the problem from developing further. You could say that what is required is repair rather than construction. From my perspective, social pedagogic practice has a closer link to construction than to repair (Storø, 2001). It is, of course, important to try to prevent problems from developing further. This will often be a vital first phase of the work. But then, when one has obtained contact with the client and achieved a common general view of the situation, it is possible to look forward. A constructionist perspective on the work with clients does not particularly concern itself with the past; rather, it is more about strengthening the client's ability to change (Parton and O'Byrne, 2000). This way of thinking enables liberation from the heavy problem narratives that, in the main, are backward-looking, and instead focuses on the client's resources, on his future and on what he needs in order to be able to manage *without* the social pedagogue (Storø, 2008). It is this phase that particularly needs a theory about constructions. The future is created, and if one feels it important that social pedagogic effort should lead to the client managing on his own, it is important to try to build the client's future with his own building materials. As expressed by Skau (2003), the helper must work in order to make himself *disposable*. Sævi (2007, p 123) talks about something that is central to this process:

> Helping a child to develop, to *become* a person who is developing, can happen because the child is understood and talked to as a person; *as if* he or she already is a person who can do things and who knows what he or she still cannot do and does not know.

In this perspective, we can say that the social constructionist-oriented social pedagogue relates to the client both as he is and as he may become.

Having said that, it is also poignant to mention that a constructionist perspective can also be useful in what I call the 'repair work', or 'repair phase' (to the extent that this can be isolated to a particular phase). The social constructionism perspective has the inbuilt assumption that understandings are something we construct. What we could call *the construction of the problem* or *the construction of how we understand the situation* will, therefore, also be an important part of the work. You could think of this in terms of the first few conversations between client and social pedagogue, where they map out what has happened, and what the client's status is and how he experiences his status. This process has room for many different social constructions. The ones you choose will be crucial for the type of action decided on.

Last in this section, I want to again mention the idea of the narrative. Berglund (2004, p 158) describes it as:

> lifting people's narratives and emphasising the social constructionist idea of social interaction and changeable identity. Human beings are not the embodiments of their own problems; problems should be regarded as cultural, social and personal ways to handle difficult life situations. The social pedagogue acts in a social and pedagogic way by teasing out alternative narratives and enabling the client to develop his narrative along new pathways. The pedagogic approach does not lock a situation down, but provides opportunities for twisting and turning – not only the situation itself, but also various alternative solutions. In this way, the client becomes a vital partner in a co-operative process with opportunities to maintain a degree of influence over the process.

Social constructionism challenges us to view the client's situation, and his work with the situation, both as individual and non-individual. The individual is maintained through a focus on each client. However, the understanding of how this person acts is linked to his participation in social collaboration. The story about his situation and its interpretation are considered important, and become a medium for collaboration between the social pedagogue and the client. The examples in this book stem mostly from individuals. The solutions that are hinted at are social. It may be considered paradoxical that work with individuals is socially oriented. What is happening is that social constructionism offers us a way to understand the client's (and everybody's) actions as fundamentally social, linguistic and negotiable – and made visible through narratives.

What does social pedagogy draw from the neighbouring sciences?

Mathiesen (2008) describes professions like psychology and sociology as neighbouring sciences to social pedagogy. It might be interesting to have a look at the neighbourly relations they have, and the kind of perspectives that social pedagogy draws from its closest neighbouring professions. I have tried to illustrate this in the model shown in Figure 2.1.

Figure 2.1: Social pedagogy's relationship to the neighbouring sciences

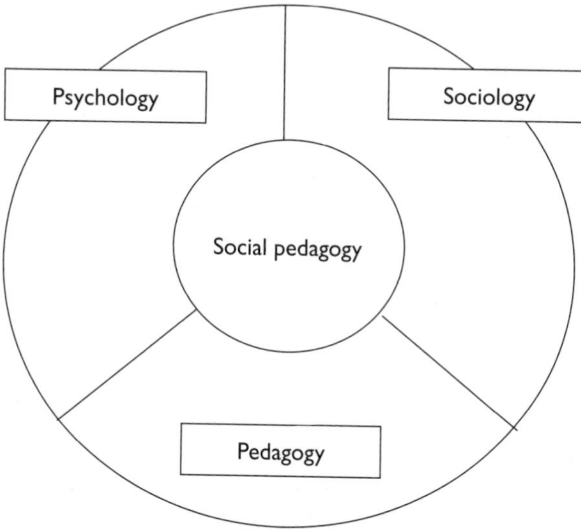

In this figure, I have presented social pedagogy as the centre of a force field between pedagogy, psychology and sociology. This picture is not without problems, for example, because it implies that the three sciences have an equally large and balanced influence on social pedagogy, which is not the case. The model also implies that the three are influencing the one, without saying anything about how social pedagogy may affect the other three. It also looks as if the three neighbours encircle and surround social pedagogy in such a way that there is no influence from other theoretical perspectives. This would also be problematic. It is obvious that, in particular, social work, criminology and theology also ought to be mentioned if this model were to be comprehensive (Mathiesen, 2008). To some extent, this type of model may be a good illustration of *some topics*; however, it also often has limitations as an explanatory model.

Nevertheless, if we explore it, it may be interesting to see what the other three contribute to social pedagogy. Starting with sociology, we can see that social pedagogy acquires an understanding of the individual's relationship to social communities. Society puts restrictions on the individual, but also provides it with opportunities – through communality. The social pedagogic understanding of a problematic upbringing – the pedagogic emergency situations – can be given explanations that stem from thinking about the community where the individual grows up. But people are not just members of a community. They are also individuals with feelings, relationships and an inner life. Psychology helps us to see these sides of a human being, the private individual, and this is what the social pedagogue largely deals with. This is where we will find the more individually oriented explanations for maladjustment – both in individuals and in relationships. The pedagogic emergency situations can also be understood as including these elements. Pedagogy has a particular position among these three professions. Strictly speaking, it isn't a neighbouring science in the same sense as the other two. If it doesn't live 'next door', like neighbours do, it lives in the same house, as a member of the same family. Pedagogy must be regarded as very closely related to social pedagogy. Its function in the model I have presented is that it provides direction for the specialist perspective in social pedagogy. It is in pedagogy that we find the very central concept of formation. The social pedagogue practitioner works with upbringing, education, change and formation. He works in a multidisciplinary field, where pedagogy is the bedrock.

To end this chapter, I will briefly mention that in most of what I am describing as psychology, I am emphasising the profession's individual perspective. However, it should be said that psychology also includes theories about the community. The strand in psychology that is probably closest to social pedagogy, namely, cultural psychology, attempts to encompass both the individual and the communal (or cultural). As an example, I could mention Gulbrandsen (2006, p 251), who stresses the importance of culture for children's psychological development. She writes that 'it is through interpersonal relationships that people develop and challenge shared systems of meaning'. The parallel to Paul Natorp's thesis that 'Man can only become Man through human interaction' (Mathiesen, 1999, p 15) is obvious. Oppedal (2007, p 287) thinks that the cultural psychology perspective challenges pedagogy by 'underlining the reciprocal influence between the individual's innate abilities and the linguistic, social and cultural resources found in the individual's surroundings. Individual and social formation can therefore not be considered independent of each other'. It is interesting that the concept of formation, which, in many ways, stems from pedagogy, is used in a psychological context. This is an indication that interdisciplinary links between social pedagogues and psychologists might be more valuable than previously assumed. Besides, it is an indication that psychology can find inspiration for perspective development in social pedagogy.

Notes

[1] This might be called the social aspect of general pedagogy (my own comment).

[2] We might also include other minorities, but it would take too long to list them all.

[3] He describes the other as 'the socialisation which takes place in schools, nurseries and families' (Madsen, 2006, p 37).

[4] Parton and O'Byrne's book deals with social work. The authors attempt to look at this profession with a constructionist view. I am using these authors as a source in several places where it has (a corresponding) relevance to social pedagogy.

[5] The term 'narrative' implies telling stories, for example, the stories the client tells about himself. I shall return to this later in the chapter and also in Chapter Seven, under the heading *Language*. The term 'salutogenic' points to the factors that give us good health (as opposed to the ones that make us ill).

[6] We could shine a critical light on the well-known Kierkegaard quote that life must be lived forwards but can only be understood backwards. From a social constructionist understanding, it would be more correct to say that we construct our understandings along the way, as we live life. It is not only a life lived (the past) that creates a basis for understanding oneself. Current actions and plans for the future also do this. Creating understandings, or meaning, can, thus, be understood as the way we live. Or, we can say that we create meaning through living.

[7] At the same time, Madsen is interested in modernity (see, eg, Madsen, 2005, p 58).

CHAPTER THREE

From theory to practice

This chapter is intended as a description of the link between theory and practice. It might equally well have been called 'From perspective to action'. All actions in social pedagogic practice are linked to theory or to a theoretical perspective, and all social pedagogic theory ought to be oriented towards the practical, towards the level of activity.

I will start the chapter with some reflections on the relationship between theory and practice in social pedagogy. Given that social pedagogy (also) is a practical profession, it is possible to identify what we might call social pedagogic methods. We can talk about the practising element of social pedagogy. The practice-oriented social pedagogue carries out his work in a way that is not arbitrary. As previously mentioned, non-arbitrary action is guided by theory. It is also guided by practical experience, which is often not written down. Through many practical situations, the practitioner develops experience, which, in itself, provides guidelines for his next practical actions. Several authors have shown an interest in this process, for example, Schön (2001), who writes that the practitioner acquires practical competence through reflecting on his own practice. Herberg and Jóhannesdóttir (2007) are interested in practice, and the kind of training social workers and social pedagogues need in order to carry out their practice. They particularly focus on the importance of reflecting on practice, through supervision, and participation in what they call 'social learning communities'. One of the most important contributions from Schön (2001) is his theorising around how practitioners (across many professions) are reflecting *while* they work. Such reflection is harder to spot than the reflection one carries out after having completed the action. My understanding of social pedagogic practice is based on Schön's concept of practice.

With his claim that practical rationality is different from technical rationality, Schön has given us an important contribution towards the understanding of practice. To simplify this, we could translate rationality as 'way of thinking'. The technical way of thinking focuses on defined problems that can be described and solved. An arithmetic problem is an example of a technical challenge. Such problems can, of course, be complex; for example, you need to make many, often complex, calculations in order to plan the construction of a large bridge. However, this does not alter the fact that all the components of a technical problem in reality are simple, because they are logical. Practical problems in fields like social pedagogy are different. Such problems cannot be solved with only logical calculations. The practical problems are often not solvable in themselves – in the sense that there is no single logical solution that can be regarded as *the final* solution to the problem. When the practitioner needs to solve a problem, he often has to choose between several apparently equally valid solutions. Therefore, the logical element grounded in technical rationality is not sufficient to be able to make the choice. When the social pedagogue practitioner makes his choices, he has to use *value-based* assessments. Relevant questions could, for example, be: 'What would be best for the person in question?', 'What is the context of the problem that needs to be understood?' and 'Which solution will serve everyone involved in the best possible way?' When answering these questions, the practitioner is faced, in particular, with two sliding assessment scales. One is founded on clinical experience, and can be formulated like this: 'What functions best based on my – or the client's – experience?' The other is based on ethical reflection, and could be formulated like this: 'What would be the ethically correct action?'

Child welfare workers often need to use their professional discretion. To use one's discretion involves exactly using a practical rationality and reflecting over which solution would be best for those involved. It is inherent in the very concept of discretion that no single solution is better than all the others. You have to choose between several alternative solutions, which may all appear to be equally valid. Child welfare legislation in Norway contains certain principles to guide the use of such discretion. The most important is the principle that all decisions shall be made in *the child's best interest*. This type of principle is an expression of value-based regulation. The use of discretion may be seen as a practical expression of a reflective practice. The reflection captures both theoretical assumptions and practical experience (cf Schön, 2001), and aims to create a synthesis out of them. The relationship between reflection and discretion is, therefore, that reflection represents the thought process where various options are considered, while using discretion demands that one also makes a decision.

However, the practitioner must also pay heed to theory. I am thinking of theory as a summary of experience, and, as such, it is important to refer to Schön in order to get a picture of how the practitioner theorises his experience. It is of particular interest to look at the practical experience the practitioner builds up *while he is practising*. According to Schön (2001), however, this building up of experience does not happen by itself. It is constructed through the practitioner's reflection on his actual practice – on his actions and what they result in. As much of this reflection happens *while practising*, Schön suggests defining the concept *reflection-in-action* as the fundamental function for gathering experience while practising. So, practical rationality consists of elements like reflection, learning from practice, having an eye for the unexpected in practical situations, constructing significant meaning from apparently different elements of the solution, improvising, and so on. The practitioner uses these functions to theorise. With that, I mean that he builds his understanding on that which functions well and that which functions less well. So, the development of a practically oriented theory starts with practice and is further developed in practice – in the reflection that happens during practice.

We can say that the practitioner constructs understandings along the way, while practising. We must, however, be careful not to romanticise this process. As a rule, practical problems also contain logical elements. At times, the logical elements can be quite prominent, and the practitioner's contribution might be the way he puts them all together into a whole. So, the constructions do not simply appear out of nothing. We can find an example of this in the architect's execution of his practice. The architect uses several logical elements (eg calculations of material strength), but good architects also exercise a type of artistry, which means that they can create constructions that nobody has seen before. Schön is particularly interested in the experienced practitioner exercising a kind of highly developed artistry that one can study – and possibly try to emulate – but where the chances of success are small unless one has personally reached the same level of experience.

Another aspect of such constructions, which is particularly evident in certain types of practice, is that the practitioner does not work on his own. This is an important point for the social pedagogue practitioner, who usually works in dialogue with others, that is, his client and his colleagues. We can therefore describe the social pedagogue practitioner not only as a constructor, but also as a social constructor. Reflection during action occurs most successfully through discussions between the various actors in practical situations. By combining Schön's (2001) notion about the practitioner and his 'reflection-in-action' with Burr's (2003) description of the concept of 'social constructionism', we get a picture of a multifaceted process of social collaboration, which contains continuous negotiations about important understandings. These understandings, in turn, form the basis for the further execution of practice, for the action element. If we add Parton and O'Byrne's (2000) 'client-centred approach', we get a picture of a practice where the client's contribution to the further development of the practice to his own best advantage is regarded as very central.

The social pedagogue practitioner knows that a broad and diverse understanding can be useful in order to practise social pedagogy. He therefore wants to work in order to develop a practical competence consisting of many elements. When working with a single client, a good social pedagogue will also focus on the client's family, friends, local environment, job/school and similar factors that may contribute to the broadest possible understanding of the problem that needs to be solved. In addition, he will try to select the appropriate course of action from as comprehensive a menu as possible within the theoretical framework.

That same evening, Trond googles Mette. He was quite curious about the woman he met in the cafe at lunchtime, and wants to know more. He finds a lecture she has given – the full version. Trond prints it out, and settles down to read it. Half an hour later he gets an idea. He has noticed one particular sentence in the lecture: 'Competence about how to act in the new media reality represents one of the most important trump cards in terms of inclusion in our society'. Trond immediately realises that his own clients, by and large, are on the outside of the context Mette talks about in this sentence. 'Marginalised', as she would probably say. He really wants to discuss this. He clicks on Mette's email address, which he found while searching, and writes: 'I find what you write very interesting, but I'm not sure how useful it is, at least for me. What you write doesn't really help me to understand what I should do when talking to someone just waking up after an overdose. I mean, that's about an individual's inner life, isn't it? What do you think, maybe we could have a chat about this some time ... over a beer maybe?'

As social pedagogic theory is so broad and there are no clear guidelines about what social pedagogic methods actually are, it can be difficult to define what social pedagogic practice is and what it isn't. However, at this stage, we can state that social pedagogue practitioners are informed (guided by theory), practice-oriented (their actions and what they lead to are, in themselves, important) and diverse (they use a wide variety of theories and methods on different levels and in different arenas). In the example of Trond and Mette's different perspectives, we can see that Trond has difficulty finding good guidance based on theory when acting in specific situations. He hints that he experiences social pedagogic theory as removed from reality; and it is true that the relationship between theory and practice in social pedagogy is a special one. It may seem as if the closer Trond gets to individual clients, the more he uses other types of theory, in particular, psychological theory. This is an example of what I mean by the crisis in the relationship between theory and practice in social pedagogy. Many practitioners are looking for an opportunity to follow the theory all the way into the practical work, all the way into what they actually do.

A broad understanding provides *the basis for action* in the social pedagogue's work, and he has a wide variety of methods at his disposal right from the start (Eriksson, 2005). We can therefore say that the practically oriented social pedagogue has both a dimension of understanding and a dimension of action at his disposal, as also stated by Gjertsen (2010). The dimension of understanding is common to both the practising and the theoretically oriented social pedagogue. However, the two may be interested in different aspects of a social pedagogic perspective. The action dimension is not shared to the same extent – at least the one that is directed towards concrete clients with different needs for help.

It is important for social pedagogue practitioners not to focus only on the individual client. Neither is what happens in the relationship that develops between him and the client the only important thing. His interest must also be directed towards the context the client lives in. To say that you are building on social pedagogic theory, you also have to take the societal level into consideration in order to understand. The client must be understood as part of a community, and a value such as inclusion in the community is an important marker for the direction of work with the client. According to Mathiesen (1999, p 37), if you forget to use social pedagogic theory when practising, there is a danger that the understanding of the problem will be individualised. Such a mistake might result in understanding the problem as mainly stemming from the morality of what the individual *ought* to do, or as an inner pathology. It is important to concentrate on the individual, but a one-sided individual focus will dilute social pedagogy's distinctive contribution. Inherent in social pedagogic theory will always be a critical look at the forces in society that affect the client's situation, for example, circumstances that turn them into clients or that maintain their client status.

This touches on what distinguishes social pedagogic practice from medical or psychologically oriented practice. In these practice fields, it is the individual, with his or her unique world of dispositions, body, thought, feelings and behaviour, that is the object. As I suggested in the last part of my descriptive definition, this is also of interest to the social pedagogue; but only as a partial perspective. In social pedagogy, *the individual in society* will always be the main interest. A body is not only a body, but a body among other bodies with a social life among others with the same sociality in a culture, within a macro context. For the psychologist, it will often be professionally right to cultivate a psychological perspective, for example, by using a particular psychological theory to solve emotional problems, most often at an individual level. For the social pedagogue, it would be useful to do almost the opposite, namely, look for applicable understanding from several perspectives. Put very simply, we could say that the psychologist works with personal biographies while the social pedagogue works with personal biographies in cooperation with other personal biographies in the context of social communities.

One field that is related to social pedagogy is social work. I am not going to spend a lot of time discussing the similarities and differences between these two. For some, this distinction is important; for others, it is not. Herberg and Jóhannesdóttir (2007) use the term 'twin fields', and claim that they have a common history, but also that they stand alone as independent fields. Both fields are developing, and these processes will presumably continue in parallel, which also means that the relationship between them will develop. But there is one obvious difference that ought to be mentioned. We see that the term 'pedagogy' is built into the basic concept of 'social pedagogy', something that is also particularly emphasised by Mathiesen (1999, 2008). Nevertheless, many will say that the social pedagogue is also, in many ways, a social worker. Maybe we can talk about the social pedagogue practitioner as a social worker with a pedagogic task. The social pedagogue's clients are, after all (first and foremost), children and young people. What both professions have in common is that they direct their interest towards practice (Herberg and Jóhannesdóttir, 2007). Social pedagogic practice is directed towards children and young people, while social work does not have this demarcation.

In her book on social work, Levin (2004, p 11) writes that 'social work is one of few professions where the practitioners have to exercise social management and control at the same time as compassionate solidarity, as is the case in child welfare and social services'. It is relatively clear that the social pedagogue practitioner is subjected to the same dilemma. Levin goes on to bring up three 'tension fields' where she thinks social work finds itself. These are: the relationship between theory and practice; the relationship between help and control; and the relationship between the individual and society. All these can be said to be equally relevant to social pedagogic practice and social work. Levin stresses that the concept 'tension field' suggests that one is unable to choose one or the other side of these dimensions. They influence and depend on each other. Besides, what is *between* the dimensions is interesting, not least because the dimensions are not static. In some professional fields, it is meaningful to talk about one or the other side of such tension fields, that is, to look at one phenomenon at a time. In social work and social pedagogic practice, this is not meaningful. Here, we find meaning in the dialectic relationship between opposites; in other words, here, we can see clear parallels between social work and social pedagogic practice.

The social pedagogue practitioner's relationship with theory

All actions can be linked to a theory. Let me put it like this: there is always someone who has had similar thoughts before. Often, someone has even written about them. Some social pedagogue practitioners still try to manage without theory. In my view, this is not to be recommended. To me, it is important that the practice we carry out should be *informed*, meaning that it should have its knowledge base in theory. Herberg and Jóhannesdóttir (2007, p 59) express something of the same: 'Using a theory is also a kind of practice, and training and experience in understanding how theoretical perspectives can throw light on a situation is required'. The social pedagogue practitioner cannot call himself a social pedagogue without linking his practice to theory. He can call himself a practitioner, but uninformed practice is *only* practice. It can, of course, consist of a lot of good work; however, it risks being governed by chance. As we saw earlier, values are important to those who work with people. For the untrained, we could say that the road from values to actions is relatively straight: the untrained act on the basis of an idea of *the good action*. The skilled social pedagogue must think differently. His starting point for the work is also values, but between the values level and the action level, we find theories and carefully considered methods for practice. This is illustrated in Figure 3.1.

In this way, those who are trained have an opportunity to give a rationale for their practice. Their practice will not be arbitrary. By using different theories, it becomes clear that they give different meaning to the phenomena they observe. It is therefore important to have an element of understanding beyond that which is purely values-based.

Referring to theory implies the need to build knowledge of different theories. Not all helpers are conscious of the theories or theoretical perspectives that underpin the choices they make when intervening. As professional social pedagogy demands broad consideration and reflection, it is extremely important to provide a full explanation of one's interventions and how they were arrived at. One ideal, which is often referred to when adopting a wide perspective, is being eclectic. Being eclectic implies gathering elements from several perspectives and then creating a meaningful new whole. When we use the expression *being eclectic*, it is obvious that we are talking about a particular attitude, possibly one that manifests itself in a manner of being. But what is eclectic *action*? We find the action element by studying various perspectives and viewing what we learn from that as a diversity of possible courses of action in particular practical situations, and then, consciously and with great consideration, choosing the course that seems right. This might mean choosing two actions or interventions based on two different theories. The real eclectic is able to explain and give reasons for his choices.

Figure 3.1: The untrained and the trained – their relationship with theory

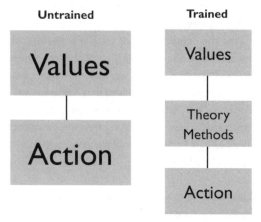

In social pedagogic practice, we often meet professionals who say they have an eclectic attitude. They show this by emphasising the importance of not getting locked into a strictly defined perspective. The reasoning will often be that it is difficult, maybe even ethically irresponsible, to explain human actions from just one perspective. Seen in this way, the positive ideal is to be found in an eclectic attitude. Saying that one works eclectically in order to avoid giving detailed reasons for an intervention is, of course, less positive. We can imagine a situation when 'professional laziness' is tolerated by referring to the concept 'eclecticism'. A true eclectic must be able to gather elements from different perspectives, and then explain what he has done. He ought to be able to explain his reasoning for choosing the various building blocks in his compound perspective. In reality, being a true eclectic is far more difficult than following one professional track.

Note that I am using the concept of 'theory' in a broader sense than many others. I do not only talk of theory as something that is written in books, but also as something that is the starting point of all our actions. For example, if a father says: "I drive my daughter to her sports club because I think it is good for her to have something to do with her friends". This father's theory is that the activity is a good one. In addition, he has a theory about the social potential of the activity. He doesn't mention a theory about the importance of exercise in order to keep fit. This could be an equally central theory, and may be the most important one for another father who drives *his* daughter to the same sports club. We would ask ourselves if physical activity carries less importance for the first father. It is by no means certain that what he *does not* talk about is not important to him. If we want to know, we have to find out – by asking. It is important to investigate each other's theories in order to learn more about the actions than the mere fact that they are carried out. Delving into the theories we have about our actions will enable us to find out more about why we act in the way we do. It will also provide us with a tool for talking to others about both the actions and the theories: a language tool. Studying theory in this way also creates opportunities for collaboration with others.

> The children's home had two contact persons. They worked shifts in order that the children should have one of them there most of the time. As a rule, this worked well, but Hanna and Vigdis, who were the contact persons for Karianne, often found that they disagreed about what needed to be done. During discussions at the meetings, they generally more or less agreed. However, when they worked individually, it turned out that they did very different things. Both of them realised that Karianne was confused by the differences. They, themselves, were frustrated by frequently ending up working in different ways, even if they had discussed something that they thought they had agreed on. They both felt that they had a close relationship as colleagues, and felt that they respected each other as professionals.
>
> During this period, their colleague, Siri, was undergoing some further training, learning about the relationship between theory and practice. For her extended essay, she chose to investigate her colleagues' cooperation problem. She decided to interview them together and get them to tell her what they felt was important in their work with Karianne. Siri made an audio recording of the interview and transcribed the material. Then she reviewed it, sentence by sentence. Siri's hypothesis was that it would be useful to look for non-spoken professional disagreement.
>
> Gradually, Siri found a pattern. Hanna's sentences often described an emotional dimension in her understanding of the kind of help Karianne needed, while Vigdis had many sentences that pointed more in the direction of Karianne's learning requirements. Siri formed a picture of the disagreement between the two colleagues as being based on their different theoretical perspectives on their work: one psychodynamic and the other to do with the theory of learning.
>
> She presented this to Hanna and Vigdis, who were very surprised. It is true that they had been aware of a certain difference in how they worked and what was important to them, but they had no idea that this could be so clearly linked to theory. Hanna and Vigdis had often realised that they put different emphases on certain phenomena; however, they perceived this more as coincidence, or possibly something linked to their different personalities, than as theory-based ideas.

The situation Hanne and Vigdis found themselves in will be familiar to many. Working with a group of colleagues, we sometimes observe differences; but we think of these mostly as expressions of different people having *their own* ways of doing things – in other words, that the personal factor is decisive. Maybe it is to a large extent, but, if so, we need to include many aspects in this 'personal factor'. This is not only about personal characteristics of individual social pedagogues, as in one being interested in deep and complex questions in the work with the children or young people and another mostly preoccupied with activities. It is also about understandings, how we deal with phenomena and events. For most people, these understandings will have traces of, or even be influenced by, different, explicit theoretical perspectives. They can have many sources, maybe fragments of one's own upbringing or one's individual values, but also books on theory one has read. In that case, we could say that theoretical perspectives, in many ways, are so deeply anchored in that person that they may be difficult to spot, not least for the person himself. Most of us have been in a situation when someone asks 'Why did you do that?', without being able to give a clear answer: 'I don't really know, it just seemed like the best thing to do …'. In such conversations, we often accept such statements. We accept that the other person is unable to explain his reasons fully. If we were more insistent and investigated more fully with the other person, we probably would be able to unearth the theories behind the choices made – whether we are talking about theories of the type that is written down in books, or theories from somebody's everyday life, which only rarely, if ever, are written down.

Siri's extended essay showed how theory is deeply embedded in us and in her colleagues at the children's home, and, at the same time, how hard it can be to spot it and formulate it. This type of investigation into the theory we use is something social pedagogue practitioners ought to carry out from time to time.

It was the anniversary of the recreation centre, and they were arranging an anniversary seminar. The manager, Lasse, wanted to take the opportunity to strengthen the staff's theoretical understanding. Working with the deputy manager, Mona, they created a scheme where all 22 employees were asked to answer some questions about what they considered to be the most important aspects of the centre, and what the people who worked there were good at. Lasse and Mona had many replies, which showed: that the staff were interested in the local environment perspective; that they regarded prevention as important; and that they were focusing on youth culture and activities. All these had been included by Lasse and Mona in the programme for the centre, and they had been discussed at a previous seminar. However, there was one aspect that they hadn't come across before. Several of the staff had mentioned working with young people from other cultures as an area that was characteristic of the centre. It was hardly surprising that a multicultural perspective was mentioned, as recent years had seen an increase in people with other cultural origins moving there. What came as a bit of a surprise to Lasse and Mona was that the staff felt that this was such an important aspect of everyday life at the centre, and that they were good at working with these people. Lasse and Mona decided to look at how this could be included in the centre programme, and agreed that they needed to do something to ensure high-quality work in this area, which they, as managers, to a certain degree had overlooked.

The alternation between carrying out actions, reflecting on them and viewing them against theory and ethics – in order to act in the light of such reflection –

can be seen as a necessary cycle for developing practice. It is important that such reflection should have a development orientation. Being interested in practice *could* also mean trying to do more of what one already masters, or what has been seen to work in previous practice. There is something positive in learning from practice, but if the learning is solely on a practical level, it becomes problematic, as it will quickly lead to doing the same things over and over again. Workplaces that attempt to think in this way will probably be able to show *some* good work in the short term, but the real spark will disappear after a while. Repetition becomes mechanical and destroys creativity. We could say that the workplace is in danger of becoming characterised by a *culture of repetition*. Few social pedagogues would agree that it is useful *only* to do more of what was done yesterday. They are keen to try to find, try to construct, new ways of working. Sometimes, this can involve working in new ways with well-known problems; other times, this can involve learning new moves because they are presented with hitherto unfamiliar problems and challenges. So, in reality, the demand for development obliges us to attempt to discover new ways of solving problems, not least because we are constantly meeting new people who need help. We cannot, however, learn in the best way until we assume real responsibility for the learning. One way to do this is to reflect on our own practice. Herberg and Jóhannesdóttir (2007) emphasise the importance of reflection in order to include ethical questions, norms and values into our professional approach. When we reflect on practice, we often try to discover *what* in the practice makes it good. As a rule, we then quickly start moving into a theoretical landscape and a values-based landscape. We might find some of this theoretical reflection in the area of everyday theory, while other reflection is in the bordering neighbouring area of academic theory. Workplaces that reflect a lot on their own practice may gradually create a *culture of reflection*.[1] Inherent in this is that it is easier to develop such a culture when there is time and space set aside for reflection, and when managers and mentors emphasise its importance.

One of the ideals of a workplace engaged in social pedagogic work is therefore to create a culture of reflection. This will enable actions and the thinking behind them to be regularly investigated in order to learn, and, in turn, bring increased understanding to how practice is carried out. However, according to Eriksson's (2005) study of social pedagogy in the Nordic countries, the practising social pedagogue does not seem to participate to any great extent in reflection on social pedagogic theory. The study suggests that social pedagogic reflection, first and foremost, happens among theoretically oriented social pedagogues and researchers. Here, then, is a challenge to the social pedagogue practitioner: include reflection in the execution of practice and use it actively to develop practice. Maybe Trond has something to learn from Mette in this respect.

Perspectivation

We have seen that when the social pedagogue works, he can become more proficient by trying to understand which theory he is using, or which theory can be linked to the action he is carrying out. We can say that the theories look at the phenomena in different ways, or that they have different perspectives on them. Some people feel that the 'action part' of what we do becomes clearer if we describe it with a verb, which may have some merit. If we are going to do so here, we could use the word *perspectivate*. Linguistically, however, this is a little cumbersome, so we normally talk about adopting one (or more) perspective(s). It is important to understand that we *choose* a perspective, we choose between different, alternative perspectives. Such choices are not arbitrary. They are guided by what we have learnt and what we consider sensible. We could also say that we construct perspectives on the basis of previous constructions. Some of the perspectives we construct are very clear to us, but others are less easy to spot. My understanding is that we need to be more conscious of the perspectives we choose.

In order to understand 'perspective' a bit better we can compare it to wearing special glasses. Imagine putting on a pair of glasses with particular characteristics, and when we do, we see the things we look at in certain ways. Imagine one colleague saying to another: "When you say that, I get the impression you have put on your problem glasses. You are not seeing the client's resources at all!" We get the idea straight away that we should also have a pair of resource glasses, to be worn frequently. At other times, multicultural glasses, poverty glasses and so on might be useful. This image shows us that we often regard and perceive only *parts* of reality. It can be both necessary and useful to adopt a partial perspective. However, it can also be problematic, unless we understand that what we see are 'only' parts of a bigger picture. Putting on a particular pair of glasses challenges us to also be conscious of which glasses we are not putting on.

We could also compare adopting a perspective to climbing a mountain, and looking at the world from the top. You have then taken a position that gives a particular perspective. Looking down on the town at the foot of the mountain could be said to be a 'top–down perspective'. From this perspective, you would see *certain* things very well (what happens on the roof terraces and in some of the streets) and other things very badly, or not at all (what goes on inside the houses). If you stand on a mountain top and say that you have a view over the town, some people would nod in recognition and agree. You can say something about the number of houses in the town, how many streets there are and where they run. You can say something about whether the town is on the coast or inland, maybe also something about its economic base. However, some people might object that too much remains unseen from this perspective to be able to call it an overview. They might say that in order to get a better perspective on what happens in the town, it is necessary to go down to it, walk around it, ring doorbells and visit those who live in the houses to see what they are doing, talk to them. *That* would have provided a different perspective. We might call it a 'near-perspective'. If we then moved into one of the houses and got a job in the town, we would be able to adopt a participating perspective, or an 'insider-perspective'.

This image contains certain parallels to qualitative versus quantitative research. These two main research methodologies deal with very different perspectives. Many would say that in modern research discourse, it is impossible to achieve a good analysis without combining different perspectives and methods. In this example, that would mean having to *both* climb up to the top of the mountain in order to look down *and* walk around the town and talk to people in order to get a sufficiently broad picture of the town.

Theories are also perspectives. Psychoanalytic theory has a perspective that implies that the individual goes through a personal development while growing up. It is as if Freud stood next to the child and followed them through the various phases, which he absolutely did not do. Nevertheless, his theory has mainly an individual perspective; and a perspective on the child; and a perspective on emotions. It says little or nothing about, for example, group processes, the social environment or ethnicity. Freud showed little interest in *such* perspectives. If we want a perspective on the social environment a child grows up in, we need to look, for example, at Bronfenbrenner's ecological model of human development. Its perspective is strongly linked to an understanding of social forces in the different layers of people's social environment. However, Bronfenbrenner's theory would clearly be inadequate as a perspective on the individual child's psychological development.

We could say that some theorists are sitting on mountain tops while others are walking the streets. In other words, they have put themselves in different positions, and describe what they see from there. They help us to understand through their descriptions. But we would be wrong if we thought that they were telling us the truth. Each of them can 'only' offer a perspective. They show us what they see, and are interested in seeing, from where they have positioned themselves. On the other hand, a perspective is not 'only'. A perspective is very useful. It tells us: 'If I stand over here I will see something useful, come and have a look, maybe you will find it useful, too'. We see that it can be an important choice to adopt other perspectives as well. This provides the opportunity to choose the one that is useful for the actions we are about to undertake. In a constructionist-oriented understanding, we can say that the constant creation of new understandings is a professional responsibility. The various understandings, or perspectives, we use are not 'ready-made packages' to be used in the same way in all situations. We must adjust the chosen understanding to the situation and the person we are working with all the time. This kind of 'tidying' up of perspectives is a constant meta-activity in the everyday professional life of the social pedagogue practitioner.

I would like to propose three ideals when it comes to perspectivation in social pedagogic work: the first is to develop a consciousness about perspectives; the second is to maintain one perspective; and the third is to be able to alternate between perspectives.

When we talk to a social pedagogue about the actions he carries out, it may be interesting to investigate whether he is conscious of his theoretical perspective. If you ask why he did what he did in a given situation, it is interesting to hear if the explanations given are linked to theory. Let us look at some possible answers to such a question. The person we ask may have perspectives such as *'I think it would be useful for that particular child'* or *'I think that children in care should spend as much time with the parents as possible'* or *'It is important for the child to learn social skills'*. If the aim is to find a theoretical perspective, then all these answers are imprecise. Let us take a closer look at them.

It is difficult to link a particular theory to the first one. It looks as if the reasoning is of a more private character (*'I think …'*). The person who says this about a child he is working with ought to be challenged to say something more about what in the change-oriented work would have been useful, why it would have been useful, in what way it would have been useful and also, preferably, which theoretical perspective he used in order to arrive at this assumption.

The second answer appears more considered. It is true that this social pedagogue says 'I think …', and that this is a pretty good indication of a somewhat private perspective. However, the private perspective is at least expressed as an opinion, and we have to believe that there is some thought behind that. We can see from the reasoning behind his opinion that it may be linked to some more general perspectives. We could hazard a guess that this social pedagogue is interested in the legislative principle about the child's best interest, maybe he has read research and theoretical literature about relational bonds between children and parents, or maybe he is more preoccupied with the child's legal rights. We do not know if the person uttering this sentence is interested in psychology or the law or maybe yet another theoretical field. If we were having a discussion with this social pedagogue, it might be prudent to ask what he means by his statement, for example, by asking: 'How do you justify your statement?' or 'What grounds do you give for your statement?' We would then find out whether he has a perspective beyond the merely private, and which of the proposed reasons (or other reasons) are important to him.

Only in the third answer do we find a hint of a clearer perspectivation. Here, the social pedagogue says that his thinking is following a theory-based norm. We see that he links his thought to a learning theory perspective, possibly a social learning perspective. If we were to ask this social pedagogue, he would probably be able to say something more about the basis for his assumption. Maybe this is a professional with a clear perspective. He would be even clearer if he, for example, said something like 'Based on learning theory thinking we ought to implement interventions that strengthen her social skills'. But we are rarely this specific, even in conversations between professionals.

So, the first ideal I would like to promote is that the social pedagogue needs to develop his consciousness about the perspectives he is using. We have seen that Siri's extended essay and Lasse and Mona's seminar preparation are two methods in this respect. Siri discovered that it can be necessary to break everything down to a sentence level in order to find the thought behind the actions. A third way of working is to introduce the practice of posing more probing questions in groups of social pedagogue colleagues. It ought to be possible to ask colleagues to expand the thinking behind suggested interventions or certain actions. It is, of course, necessary to do this in a positive way. The idea is not to instigate a culture of inquisition. Colleagues should not be confronted in order to be 'caught' if what they say is not coherent. Rather, we should try to develop a positive climate where one shows an interest in the reasoning of others, that is, their perspectives. Some useful questions in this respect might be:

- What was the thinking behind this?
- What is important to you when you suggest this?
- How have you arrived at what you are saying?

Or maybe:

- Which theory are you applying when you say that?

Having arrived at a perspective, one is often faced with new challenges. There are many ways of regarding a problem; therefore, there must also be many ways of solving it. Perhaps there is a sudden realisation of the need to think in a different way in a specific situation. In a staff group, different people often pull the discussion in different directions. Those who have been members of a staff group for a period of time will have seen some colleagues clinging to their perspectives, while others change theirs from time to time. Both holding on to one perspective and alternating between several can be positive contributions to the group's discussions. Both can also have the opposite effect, by preventing debate. I will come back to both these ideals, but first let me say something about being decisive as opposed to being indecisive.

Working in social pedagogic workplaces, you are often faced with situations where you have to choose *what* to do, and also *if* you should do anything. If you see two children having an argument, it will sometimes be right to intervene; other times, it will be better to let them sort it out themselves. It is important for the social pedagogue to develop a strong consciousness about his own thinking on this: 'Should I act or should I not?' This is a step in the direction of developing reflection about the next step: 'Why do I make the choice that I make?' In a practical situation like this, you are only two questions away from the theory. The road need not be any longer. Let us go back to the example with the two children having an argument. Here is some background information:

One afternoon at the school day-care facility, Bjørn notices that Sofie and Nasreen are pushing each other, obviously having an argument. Bjørn cannot hear what they are saying as he is standing a few metres away, and there is a lot of noise around him. His first thought is that this is something they need to sort out themselves, but he nevertheless chooses to observe what is happening. Nasreen hits out. It is clearly quite hard, because Sofie falls over. Bjørn decides to intervene, and calls out: "Hello, what are you two doing?" He then starts moving towards the girls.

What interests me most in this episode is Bjørn's level of consciousness. At first, he decides not to do anything about what he is observing. But when the episode starts developing in a negative direction, he reverses his decision. He intervenes. Both decisions seem sensible, based on the situation at the time. Bjørn made two conscious choices, and acted accordingly. At no time was he a passive observer of the situation. *That* might well have been a third alternative. So, Bjørn had the following alternatives: (a) decide not to do anything about it; (b) not to decide whether he should do anything about it; and (c) decide to do something about it. Bjørn can only be said to have made a real assessment in the first and last alternative. The three alternatives are placed side by side in Figure 3.2.

Figure 3.2: Three alternative actions measured in terms of the level of consciousness

a) Decide not to do anything about it	b) Not decide whether to do anything about it	c) Decide to do something about it
High level of consciousness	Low level of consciousness	High level of consciousness

In this figure, the two favourable alternatives are on the left and on the right. Not because we are able to predict the outcome (we don't know anything about that from this little story), but because both of them are founded on conscious decisions. The professional's action in alternatives a) and c) was to make a reasoned decision. It is true to say that this thinking happened very quickly, almost intuitively, but it was there. The alternatives in the middle and on the right of the figure both entail Bjørn *not* intervening, that is, the same result as far as action is concerned. However, they have a very different foundation. We do not know enough to judge Bjørn's actions at the different times, but we should give him credit for making conscious decisions on both occasions. It looks as if Bjørn chose one perspective, and then another when the situation demanded it. Ideally, he would also have been able to explain more about what he was thinking when he chose what to do and then link his explanation to theory.

Let us go back to the second ideal, the one about sticking to one perspective. Everyday life in a professional social pedagogic environment can appear quite chaotic. Prioritising can sometimes be difficult in the stream of events and people's varying assessments of them.

We are now going to visit a youth residential centre where we sit down at the staff handover meeting. The day staff are on their way home, while the evening staff are planning the evening.

> Tine, a milieu worker who is the contact person for Marius, has planned to talk to him that evening about why he has been playing truant the last couple of days. At the handover, she mentions this, and adds: "I'm going to put a little pressure on him, getting to school is no problem for him if only he wanted to." Her colleague, Anders, frowns deeply: "When I spoke to him yesterday I gathered he was very upset about the argument he had with his mother over the weekend, so I'm not sure you should put a lot of pressure on him about this today. Might be better to plan to have a nice evening together instead." "Actually, I agree", says Rolf, who is on his way home after a day shift, "he seemed quite upset this morning, but I think it was mostly to do with his worsening relationship with his teacher after playing truant so often." Tine sighs; she can see that the other two have a point. She still believes in being strict with Marius now and confronting him. Her thinking is that the consequence of not dealing with problems is that they just get worse.

This little discussion about working with Marius reflects the diversity of interpretations that is often present in a group of colleagues involved with children or young people. Furthermore, not only are there several interpretations, but those who interpret are themselves participants in the environment where the interpretations take place. This often makes it even more difficult to 'keep a clear head'. In such situations, it would probably have been liberating to climb up a mountain and view the whole thing from above.

It is obvious that Tine does not really want to hear several explanations about why Marius is upset. She is more interested in getting him going. 'Consequences' is a key word in her thinking. Maybe her perspective is 'consequence pedagogic', while her colleagues tend more towards psychological explanations? If Tine is going to be able to work well with Marius this evening and beyond, she needs to make a few choices. One choice can be to stick to her original perspective. If that is what she decides to do, it naturally needs to be with her colleagues' agreement.

We also see that the discussion at this handover meeting is not particularly founded on theory. At least it is not obvious that the various viewpoints are guided by theory. The supervisor brings this up the following week when Tine asks that this particular handover meeting should be the topic for the next full staff meeting.

> Tine starts by recapping the situation. She says that she felt quite unable to act when her shift started that evening. She thought she had support for the plan that they had set up together for working with Marius two months earlier. That was why she began the handover by saying that she wanted to put some pressure on him.
>
> The supervisor asks Tine, but also the two colleagues who spoke up, to say something about the theoretical perspective on which their statements were founded. Tine maintains that she was mostly interested in regarding the work she was doing with the boy in the light of humanist-existentialist thinking, with a focus on his own choices. She thinks it was important for him to learn to face the consequences of his choices.

She felt she was therefore also oriented towards the social learning inherent in the situation. Tine says that it is important for the boy to enter social arenas where he can interact with other young people. She is worried that he will otherwise not have sufficient opportunities to acquire norms and social skills, which he will need in future interaction with people of his own age. When the supervisor turns to Rolf, he looks down and says that he does not really know which theory he was using, only that he had observed that the boy was upset and he thought it was an important piece of information. Anders, on the other hand, has a more reflected reason for his understanding. He says that he has been preoccupied with Marius's relationship with the person who could be most clearly defined as a 'significant other' for the boy. Anders feels that all the talk about consequences and choices is futile as long as this relationship remains difficult. He feels that his perspective is founded on a psychodynamic basic understanding.

The supervisor gives the staff a challenge based on these perspectives. She thinks they need to work out which perspective they should choose as the most important one in the work with the boy. "Maybe it will be possible to find combinations", she says, but she does not think they ought to expose him to the 'perspective-hopping' that emerged at the staff meeting. She tells Rolf that she thinks he should continue offering his observations, but that he also ought to try to place what he sees in a clear framework of understanding. Rolf nods in agreement.[2]

This discussion could clarify the picture for these colleagues. It is difficult to say if this will make it easier or more difficult to choose a perspective. However, after this staff meeting, the choices ought to be better considered. This will probably also mean that the staff can be united in a more holistic understanding and holistic actions.

It may look as if the interventions in the planning of the work with Marius agreed by this staff group are not very strongly focused on practice. When we went in and observed them at an arbitrary point in time, we saw that their professional discussions were not about how best to organise the work for the shift that was about to start – in the light of what they had agreed. They seemed to be more engaged in discussing which was 'the best' perspective. It also seemed as if each of the participants tried to promote *their own* special interests. Nothing much will be achieved in a staff group that spends a lot of time discussing perspectives during the time they *really* should have been working with the client. Such situations are not very good for clients, who will find themselves at the receiving end of social pedagogic choices pointing in many different directions.

In Tine's workplace, it looks as if the management understands the importance of developing the staff's ability to reflect on their own professional practice. To that end, they have also appointed a supervisor. This gives hope that Tine and her colleagues can move on from a situation where the various perspectives compete with each other, to making choices about sticking to one perspective guiding their practice. In the story about the work with Marius, it is easiest to spot social pedagogic theory in Tine's argumentation. She is oriented towards learning in social situations, and interested in the boy's relationship with others. What she says has both a social and a pedagogic perspective.

I also promised to throw some light on a third ideal concerning perspective, namely, the ideal of being able to alternate between two perspectives. This can be viewed as another aspect of what I have just described. It is important to be able to both maintain one perspective and alternate between perspectives. Maybe Anders was right? Maybe his idea of what was important in the work with Marius was something that ought to be followed up? If so, it would be best to ask Anders to raise his doubts about the perspective that, after all, had been chosen for the work with Marius at another time and in a different situation from a handover meeting at the beginning of a shift. Instead, he should have noted down his thoughts and reverted to them at the next meeting when the plan for the work with Marius was to be evaluated. The ideal of alternating between perspectives presupposes a clarification of one's perspectives, through professional reflective conversations.

Let us fast-forward to the meeting where the plan is to be evaluated, two months after the staff meeting we have just witnessed. Anders chose to take the advice about setting aside his perspective for the time being, and they have been working according to the plan that was originally agreed – meaning that during this time, Tine has been working with the perspective in *this* plan. The staff have been working with Marius for four months and it is time to evaluate the work and make plans for the next period.

Anders has followed the advice about postponing the presentation of his perspective of what is required in the work with Marius. The manager has also asked him to present a reasoned proposal for a change in the action plan in cooperation with Tine. The two of them have been making preparations together, looking at what has happened to Marius during the period that they have been working with him. They agree that it has been important to have the whole staff behind them in this work. Tine has gradually understood the significance of bringing in other perspectives, and at the meeting, they present a plan about focusing more on the relationship between Marius and his mother during the next phase. The hard work involved in getting him to go to school has paid off, and it is now time to look at other aspects.

When the ideals stretch from maintaining one perspective to alternating between perspectives, we need to expand a little on what is good practice in this area. Combining the consideration of both ideals puts us on the trail of good practice. This *may* seem contradictory. My proposal is that the colleagues agree about using a limited number of perspectives.[3] In this way, they take into account both the demand for consistency, clarity and predictability and the demand for acquiring a certain breadth of understanding. The social pedagogic workplace where employees agree to use a limited number of perspectives takes the complexity of this practice field seriously, and acts accordingly. At the same time, they keep an eye on the diversity in social pedagogy. This way of doing things gives rise to an important opportunity: the agreement can be evaluated, renegotiated and renewed. In other words, the staff can evaluate their own practice, regularly or irregularly. We could say that perspectives are exchangeable. However, they should only be set aside when they, at the same time, can be exchanged for others, after a proper evaluation of which are the most useful.

Something else needs to be mentioned in this context. The ideal of knowing one's perspective goes for both the individual and group levels. The individual social pedagogue needs to investigate his own perspective and develop it. The staff group must do the same, and they need to do it together. Bastøe et al (2002) emphasise free dialogue as an instrument of common reflection in a collegial group. Through such processes, the group's experiences can be 'systematised, formulated and documented' (Bastøe et al, 2002, p 107). If a collegial group is to ensure good reflective processes, it must strive for open dialogue and an interest in individual perspectives. It must also put aside time and space for such reflection.

Interventions

One possible answer to the question 'What is social pedagogic practice?' is that it constitutes interventions. In other words, social pedagogic practice arises and is made visible through the interventions initiated by the social pedagogue. In this context, to intervene means to step in and do something. The intervention is the very core of social pedagogic practice. This is the professional's tool, the tool he can use when he has analysed the situation, assessed the needs of the person needing help in the actual situation and collated this with the theory and the empirical data he, as a specialist, has access to.[4]

The social pedagogue intervenes in the lives of his clients in order to facilitate change. This could be a change of behaviour, ways of relating to others, ways of thinking about one's own situation and so on. According to Madsen (2006, p 220), 'social pedagogic practice is based on visible interventions in other people's lives in order to create development, participation and learning'. What distinguishes social pedagogic practice from other forms of practice in the work with people who need help is that it seeks to encompass both a focus on the subject, social understanding and a pedagogic intention. Such intervention may be direct or indirect, directed towards the client himself or his environment, or both. The intervention can arise in different ways. Maybe the social pedagogue himself becomes aware of problems after having observed the client, and chooses to intervene. As a rule, this happens through dialogue with the client. Or it could be the actual client, or someone in his immediate environment or social network, pointing to the problems that require intervention.

The need for action

As I see it, the social pedagogue must be *willing* to intervene. This may seem obvious, but it is not always clear in the social pedagogue's practical, professional work. The need for action is not discussed much in the literature about the social pedagogue's professional practice. In *Work ethic guidelines for child welfare pedagogues, social workers and social educators in Norway* (FO, 2002), we can read a lot about *how* the actions should be carried out, with particular emphasis on the fact that they should be guided by certain values. However, the document takes it for granted that the professional practitioner actually does utilise his opportunities for intervention.

The need for action is triggered when the social pedagogue has discovered a need for help in a client, and made an assessment of what is needed to remedy the situation. It must be assumed that the social pedagogue then uses his professional knowledge and translates it into one or several interventions intended to be in the client's best interest. These days, most people would claim that the action should be designed in collaboration with the client (FO, 2002). This is an important ideal, which should be followed as far as possible. However, it does not exempt the social pedagogue from acting on his own. Expectation of this professional action can come from several points. The social pedagogic professional environment, that is, colleagues, ought to be able to expect action. Society, understood as both the client's immediate environment and society at large, ought to have a similar expectation. The expectation could be formulated as: 'This is what social pedagogues are for.' The sentence is meant to express a confidence that society can count on the social pedagogue to solve the problems that he is trained to solve. Even if he can't solve them, he must at least try.

Last, but not least, *the client* must be able to expect action. In many cases, the client has put his life in the hands of the social pedagogue, and must be able to expect the helper to have the right professional competence (Skau, 2003). If nothing is done where there is a need for action, the client might believe that action is not necessary. This could have a very negative outcome.

Ethics is more preoccupied with the consequences of the choices made by the social pedagogue in his professional activity, and, thus, about the actions he carries out, than with whether he actually acts at all. But the question of intervention versus non-intervention must still be regarded as one of the most central ethical dilemmas. The legitimacy of the whole profession is at stake in this dilemma. As long as we invest in social pedagogues, we also should expect them to do the job in the fields where they have particular specialist knowledge and competence. If the choice not to carry out an action is to be justifiable, it needs to be explained just as well and communicated just as clearly. Child welfare workers are sometimes criticised for not having intervened in families where children are at risk. In such cases, we ought to expect them to be able to explain why they chose not to do something.

The need for action is currently under pressure. The increased thinking that users should be participants in the helping process can, in some cases, result in the misconception that social pedagogic action is unnecessary unless requested by the client. In other words, you can be misled to believe that only the interventions the client (the user) himself wants are good interventions. This understanding is too narrow, as confirmed by Skau (2003). The need for action from the social pedagogue is triggered by his professional competence, which he has acquired through training and experience, and it is meant to benefit the client. If he does not use it, he is letting the client down. It is as if a dentist should decide not to use the drill because the patient did not want to feel pain. The dentist's need for action leads to him having to tell his patient that drilling is necessary, even if the patient expresses his reluctance. The question of the social pedagogue's need for action is far more complex than the meeting of an immediate need. The need for action also touches on the question of power and the execution of power.

When the social pedagogue intervenes in the lives of others, the best-case scenario is new opportunities for the people in question. Such an intervention will often be about seeing new opportunities that the client has been looking for over a long period. We might even put 'new' in inverted commas. Quite frequently, the suggestions from a wise social pedagogue build on what the client himself has done previously. The social pedagogue might be able to see things differently from the client, and the proposal may thus present itself in an entirely new light. Such processes can be described as reconstructing the client's constructions. It is important for the social pedagogue practitioner to understand that the intervention does not always need to be spectacular and completely different from anything else that has been considered and done. It does, however, need to start with a synthesis of the client's needs and his own assessment, the actual situation the client finds himself in, an overview of the opportunities and limitations available, and the practical and theoretical knowledge that the social pedagogue can contribute. Social pedagogic interventions are truly built on a combination of many factors. If these are assembled into an understanding and some concrete proposals that appear 'new', the client will have access to opportunities for change.

Interventions can take many forms:

- Rita starts a conversation group at the recreation centre with a few girls who are not asserting themselves with the other girls. She is hoping to bring the girls closer together and strengthen their social competence.
- Leif hands in a proposal for a decision on a support person for a 16 year old he has been working with for a while. The aim is to help the boy to get out more and not just sit in front of a computer all day.
- Merete initiates a system for self-registration of negative behaviour for one of the youths at the residential home. The aim is for the girl to become aware of how often she hurts others, and that the increased self-awareness will modify this behaviour.

- Cihan enters into a contract with a supervisor who is going to give guidance to several foster homes in the region. As several of the foster homes he is responsible for have young people around 16 years of age living there, he wants them to start working in the best possible way with the transition of these young people to an independent life.
- Øystein decides to read aloud a couple of times a week to some of the children at the day-care facility for schoolchildren, where he works. One of the teachers has told him that several of the children have poor reading skills, and he wants to contribute to increasing their joy of reading.
- Lindis has started preparing the presentation of a case to the County Social Welfare Board concerning a possible care order. She hopes that this will finally create a safe everyday life for the twins she has been working with during the past year.
- June hangs a climbing rope in the big tree in the corner of the play area at the nursery school. This is where she plans to bring together some of the most unruly boys in a common activity. Her goal is to let them practice waiting their turn and other social skills every day after lunch.

The client's new opportunities can be found in the intervention itself. The point is that 'someone', in this case, of course, the social pedagogue, initiates a positive process of change on his behalf. However, the situation also has inbuilt problems. It is not obvious that the intervention that is being carried out is in the client's best interest. There are often many different opinions as to what is best. Later, I will look at certain elements and try to show why interventions can be assessed in different ways.

Preferences based on different roles and tasks

When people in different roles linked to the helping process assess what needs to be done, they will often arrive at different conclusions. In this context, the most obvious example is that the helper and the person who needs help may have different views on the situation. They have two, quite distinct, roles, which could be said to be complementary. The role of the helper is partly characterised by positive values like openness towards to other person, empathy and initiative. At the same time, the helper exercises power and control (Skau, 2003). The person needing help has traditionally been described as the receiver, the owner of the problem, the one who is (more or less) ready for change. The classic use of the term is *a person in need of help who is receiving help from a helper* (Johanssen et al, 1965). This image has altered radically in the past 20 years. We can find important characteristics of their positions in the span between the 'old' and the 'new' ways of regarding helper and client.

The different roles further imply that those who own them have different tasks. Traditionally, we have tended to give the person needing help the task of formulating the problem, and the helper the role of carrying out interventions to remedy it – often after the person needing help has produced his own, authoritative formulation of what the problem 'really' is. In this image, the helper is the active part, while the one being helped is a passive receiver. In the modern version, to a greater extent, we regard the one needing help as an active contributor to the helping process, that is, in what is often called an actor perspective (Williams et al, 1999; Storø, 2003). This involves both the task of formulating the problem, finding solutions to remedy it and, perhaps in particular, an expectation that the person who is going to be helped is active in the actual process of working for change. This is true for several professional fields of practice, but it is probably particularly evident in a constructionist-oriented practice.

We see that the roles in the helping process and the tasks assigned to the roles are different. It is interesting, therefore, to see what the people who own the different roles feel about the interventions. Let us imagine that the helper proposes or initiates an intervention that demands quite an effort from the person needing help. Maybe they can both see that the proposa,l in itself, is a good one, but it is not equally certain that the one needing help is motivated or feels able to do the necessary work.

> Tine is employed as a milieu therapist in a school. She is working with Truls, who is 12. He never does any homework, and this has led to him being behind the others in the class. His teacher also reports that Truls is more isolated in the class environment than previously. Tine has decided to try to help him to better connect to both schoolwork and fellow pupils. One of the interventions she proposes is that Truls should get help with his homework. However, Truls is reluctant. He says he understands that something needs to be done, but he is fed up with schoolwork.

It is also interesting to look at other roles that help to define the context in which a helper encounters a person needing help. The latter will have people around him in roles such as mother, father, siblings, grandparents, neighbours, support persons and so on. All these various roles have their own starting points for evaluating the interventions that are proposed or initiated.

> Tine has asked for a conversation with Truls' parents. Here, she raises the question of help with homework, and suggests that the parents assume some responsibility for this by checking that their son has done his homework. The parents are reluctant. They feel that they have enough to do, and say that they think it is the job of the school to solve the problem with the boy's learning.

The question of who should do what is a central one in the practice of social pedagogy. It is particularly in this area that we experience the various actors evaluating the interventions differently. We can also see that there may be a difference of opinion about what constitutes the right intervention. In the argumentation of Truls' parents, we see that they regard the school as the central place for learning, and they seem to think that the right intervention needs to happen there.

So, we can say that the evaluation of interventions partly stems from the different roles and tasks given, and also from each actor's relationship with the helping process.

Individual preferences

When the social pedagogue assesses whether it is right to intervene, and which intervention is best, his personal or individual preferences play a part. In other words, the interventions depend to a certain extent on the person. They are founded on judgement and experience. One helper may have had good experience with individual interventions and his work is mostly directed towards the individual, while another prefers working in groups, or maybe with social networks.

> Before Tine starts the work with Truls, she talks to a colleague whom she knows has good experience with involving a pupil's parent(s) when a new intervention is to be initiated. In this way, she may benefit from experience she hasn't had herself when she starts the homework support. Tine thinks this is a good idea, having found the parents' willingness to do something pretty lukewarm during their conversation when she met them.

The individual social pedagogue's preferences are a starting point for action, for the intervention. Such preferences can, however, also limit professional practice. The helper needs to know his personal preferences and allow himself to go beyond these in order to create a wider professional evaluation.

Situational assessment

The situation in which help is to be given is always an important factor. Some will prefer the term 'context', and they might say that a contextual assessment is important in order to choose the right intervention.

The situation, or the context if you prefer, in which the person needing help finds himself contains decisive elements that influence the choice of intervention. What are these elements? They are all conceivable aspects that define the actual situation. On what we could call a 'person level', it might be about who is participating, where the situation takes place, the relationships between the participants and the aim of the actions that are being carried out. On a practical level, the physical framework conditions play a part: the budgetary situation, building design and so on. On a more general level, socio–economic, social and cultural elements will influence the situation. Contexts are not defined, separate, phenomena, but complex sets of circumstances that contain different types of social activity and that contribute to the activity of those who participate in the situation (cf Reichelt, 2006). All situations are linked to other situations that are happening at the same time, before or after, and it can therefore be difficult to assess what is important in a given situation. Situational assessments have a clear element of discretion.

> One day, Truls' form teacher tells Trine that he wants to wait a little before initiating homework help for Truls, as there are only two weeks until the Easter holiday. He thinks it would be better to begin when the pupils have returned to school after the break.

We see that the actors in a situation can evaluate it very differently. Truls's form teacher argues that the situation 'after the holiday' is more suitable for initiating the intervention for homework help than the situation 'before the holiday'.

Different initial perspectives

Another scenario is that different helpers may have different perspectives on their action. It could be a theoretical perspective, or a less rigid system of thought based on experience. A theoretical perspective will be able to create a platform from which reflection about the intervention will stem. As I have mentioned earlier, the relationship between theory and practice is largely about understanding phenomena at different levels of abstraction. Practice can, therefore, be understood as the realisation of thoughts. If we are talking about a less rigid system of thought (as opposed to a well-formulated theory), it will often not be particularly explicit, and the person thinking these thoughts may not have formulated them into technical concepts. In such cases, we are talking about something close to *individual preferences*. It might still be possible to find a clearer reasoning if we sit down with the helper who bases his work on this. Maybe he would then be able to formulate something that reflects a coherent train of thought, in which case, we could talk about a process where tacit knowledge is made audible (not least for the one who 'owns' it) by formulating it. I am in favour of such processes of formulation. In recent years, the concept of 'tacit knowledge' has acquired a certain status in several practice-oriented professions. But, in my view, there are few good arguments against formulating this knowledge.

It will often be easier to collaborate with others if the helper's perspective is made explicit. This is precisely an argument for working from a limited number of perspectives.

> Tine recently attended a course about cognitive techniques for change, and is thinking about this perspective when she is about to start the work with Truls. This means that she quickly hones in on the boy's school effort when evaluating what will be the right intervention. Talking to her colleague who is oriented towards social network theory, she is reminded that the case can look completely different from this perspective.

Through dialogue between colleagues, it will be possible to look for the best intervention in the given situation. This search is easier if the colleagues can also say something about the thinking behind the proposal they bring to the discussion.

The right time

The expression 'The right measure at the right time' has frequently been used in a social pedagogic context in the last few years. This suggests that regardless of how good an intervention is, it has to come at the right time if it is to be effective. Timing is everything. It is not very difficult to agree with these expressions, which might be a sign that they are too general to be used as technical terms. We therefore need to be more specific in our explanations of them.

The understanding of 'the right time' is an understanding of a situation where the time dimension is the part of the situation that we focus on. The situation, as it is at a given point in time, must be optimal in order for an intervention to be effective. In the opposite case, we might imagine situations where many elements are in place, but not the decisive one — at a particular time. When Truls's form teacher wanted to wait with the homework help until after the holiday, it was an expression of a point of view that 'the right time' is an important aspect of an understanding of the situation.

We can also imagine that the time dimension is to do with giving the actors in the helping process *sufficient time*. Sometimes, the social pedagogue may have a good intervention proposal, but postpone the initiation of it to give the client time to get used to the idea that something new is going to happen.

Truls' form teacher offers to have a conversation with him before the break to tell him that homework help will be initiated when they return to school. In that way, he hopes to help make Truls feel more involved in the work that the school is doing with him.

When a client is given *sufficient time*, this also increases the possibility that he will be able to motivate himself for what is to come. In other words, if the social pedagogue initiates interventions without giving the client sufficient time to take part in the change, he risks the client opposing the intervention.

Primary and secondary tasks

When working with children and young people, there are many tasks to grapple with. Some of them are directly linked to the contact with individual children/ young people; for example, conversations, activities, comforting, mealtimes and so on. Other tasks concern practical and other circumstances around the situation where the relationships take place. These might be tasks in connection with the administration of an institution, budgeting, report-writing, guidance and development of professional methods. Larsen (2004) distinguishes between primary and secondary processes. This is about the same division. The two types of work processes involve two different types of task. In this way of categorising tasks, the primary processes and primary tasks are given priority. It tells us that the direct work with children and young people is the social pedagogue's most important task. But the secondary tasks must not be forgotten. Working with them enables the work on the primary tasks.

A way to behave

As we reach the end of this chapter, I am going to return to Eriksson (2005, p 65). She introduces an alternative view of social pedagogy:

> This would mean that there is no single superior social pedagogic theory, but rather an attitude or a common values base that highlights democratic principles, and which sees society and each individual as resources in a constantly on-going process of change.

Eriksson is trying to replace the search for theoretical clarity with another concept, namely, *attitude*. She talks, in other words, about the way the social pedagogue behaves. I see this as pointing to a values-based standpoint. I consider Eriksson's suggestion as an attempt to find something common to social pedagogy, something of a more theoretical character, and that she does not find this in the theoretical landscape, but in a values-based way of doing things linked to the theory. She gives us her interpretation of how the theory should be used. To this, we can add Holst's (2005, p 19) conclusion that social pedagogy today contains three positions: the first is philosophically oriented; the second, sociological; and the third is oriented towards practice: 'a third position, where the starting point is social pedagogy as a specialist field and a profession, whose task it is to contribute to the integration in society of people who are socially threatened'. It is this last orientation that we shall explore in the next few chapters.

Date: Friday, 18 Apr 2008, 11:07:23
  From: Mette Grevstad
  To: Trond Frantsen
  Subject: Re: Hello author!
  Hi, Trond. Of course I remember. I enjoyed it. I only hope I didn't upset you with my response. I didn't really feel like having a discussion that day, just wanted to look at the book.
  What you are saying is interesting. I have to admit that I don't spend a lot of time on the problems you mention. Please don't misunderstand. I think what you do is both important and interesting. But my interest is more linked to understanding structures and overall connections. From what you are saying, I gather you have been doing some brainwork in order to understand my argumentation in the

book. Great that you bought it, now I have at least one reader :-) Nobody else has challenged me on the question you raised. I mean, the usefulness of the kind of writing that I do is probably seen as more academic and theoretical than useful for individuals. At the same time, I feel like responding to your challenge. What does theory mean to you, and what does it mean to me? It would be fun to continue our discussion.

Next week, Thursday is the only good day for me. 7pm is fine. I know the place, used to go there when I was a student.

See you soon!

MG

Notes

[1] The terms 'culture of repetition' and 'culture of reflection' are drawn from Erik Larsen and Mats Marnell's series of seminars 'Prosess og Profil' ('Process and profile'), which were held under the auspices of Oslo barnevernkontor (child welfare department) in 1984.

[2] Grønvold (2000) provides an overview of different perspectives for milieu therapy practice.

[3] I have learnt to think in this way through my colleague Erik Grønvold.

[4] I would like to reiterate my understanding of the concept of intervention, which I described in the first chapter. I made it clear that my intervention concept must not be combined with seeing the client as passive, as 'exposed to the social pedagogue's interventions'. My intervention concept presupposes that the interventions demand activity from the client.

CHAPTER FOUR

Who is the social pedagogue?

No profession has a monopoly on the title 'social pedagogue'. In this book, I have mostly thought about the child welfare pedagogue, but social educators, child and youth workers, social workers, teachers, and pre-school teachers work with some of the tasks I am describing. Besides, there are many non-professionals who might benefit from reading the book.

Instead, let us try to work out who the social pedagogue is by looking at some of the roles he may assume, and some of the work he does. Above all, I want to focus on what the social pedagogue does, and on what he does that may be similar to what other professionals do.

What is the social pedagogue?

Is the social pedagogue a social worker?

Yes, you could say that. A social worker is engaged in tasks that concern helping people who have one or more problems and who need help from others to solve them. Herberg and Jóhannesdóttir (2007, p 15) clearly state that social work and social pedagogy 'have a common area of interest: namely practice'. Some would say that the social worker is the generalist, that is, he works with all groups of people who need help, while the social pedagogue has limited his professional field to working with children and young people. Many social pedagogues also work with adults, but they are usually the parents of the children and young people who are the primary clients. As I have mentioned previously, we can regard the social pedagogue as a social worker with a particular pedagogic orientation in his work. Herberg and Jóhannesdóttir (2007) particularly hold out Jane Addams and Mary Ellen Richmond as the senior professionals in both fields, while they regard Paul Natorp as the special pioneer of social pedagogy.

Is the social pedagogue a teacher?

Yes, the role and tasks of a teacher are also represented in the social pedagogue's everyday working life. The very term gives us an idea of pedagogic, or educational, activity. The pedagogic aspect of social pedagogy has been central ever since it was described by pioneers like Natorp (Mathiesen, 2008). But the social pedagogue is not a pedagogue in the same way as the teacher in the classroom. The social pedagogue's pedagogic tasks have closer links to upbringing and formation (cf Madsen, 2006) than to school pedagogy. It is true that modern pedagogic thinking includes elements other than pure education, as when Wivestad (2007) talks about pedagogy as (both) upbringing and teaching. However, schools are still the most important arena in *that* respect. The general pedagogue, that is, the teacher, is engaged in teaching (with elements of social pedagogic practice), while the social pedagogue is engaged in upbringing (with elements of traditional pedagogy). The teacher's focus is on children, young people *and* adults generally, while the social pedagogue's focus is on children and young people in social emergency situations (Mathiesen, 1999; Madsen, 2006).

The social pedagogue's pedagogy is social by nature; the learning takes place in everyday social situations – in ordinary, everyday life. The subjects for learning are the skills, values and attitudes that are useful in the social life each individual has to live. Occasionally, this also takes place in specially arranged situations, containing elements of the general, as normally embodied by institutions. Some teachers might protest at this and claim that they teach a lot more than dry, concrete facts – including in the classroom. This is not an unreasonable objection. It only goes to show that the general teacher also has social pedagogic ambitions. Nevertheless, it is important to distinguish between the social pedagogic aspect of what the general teacher does and the social pedagogic activity carried out by the social pedagogue. The former is an aspect of acquiring knowledge, the latter, we could say, is *learning about life, in life*. I am inventing this distinction not in order to raise barriers between professional fields, but in order to clarify what the different professional groups actually do. Only when we understand that, can we collaborate and develop a common professional effort.

We have seen that the social pedagogue can be understood as a social worker with a pedagogic aim for his work, but also as a pedagogue with a social angle on pedagogy – a socially oriented pedagogue. Exactly: a social pedagogue. There must be something in this word constellation. But let us continue, and investigate other aspects of the social pedagogue's work.

Is the social pedagogue a psychologist?

The answer must be 'no'. The psychologist is engaged in treatment. The treatment is primarily directed towards maladjustment in an individual's inner psychological landscape. The social pedagogue is more of a social worker who works with the person and his life conditions seen as a whole. The psychologist has far more clearly defined knowledge and competencies than the social pedagogue. One of the tasks of a clinical psychologist is to come up with a diagnosis. This demands knowledge that can be validated.

On the other hand, psychology is a profession that constitutes an important pillar of the theoretical knowledge in social pedagogy. The social pedagogue needs to acquire knowledge about development psychology in order to be able to work with children and young people. He can then use this knowledge to distinguish between normality and deviation in what people do and how they feel. He can use it to understand how individuals and groups of people behave. And he can use it to understand the inner world of the clients he is working with, and how people project their emotions onto each other. He can also use knowledge about psychology to understand social processes in groups. However, knowledge about psychology must always be located in a wider framework if it is to be useful for the social pedagogue.

Another point worth mentioning is that the psychologist and the social pedagogue, right from the start, have a fundamentally different way of looking at a client's problems. As shown by Nyqvist (2004), there is a marked difference between understanding youth violence as an inner pathology, and, thus, a deviation from normality, and understanding it as disempowerment, 'outsiderness' and being different. Where the traditionally oriented psychologist would treat the deviation, the social pedagogue would think more in terms of the young person's lack of dialogue with the adult world, with society's institutions and with the cultural norms in the young person's environment.

Is the social pedagogue a sociologist?

Again, the answer must be 'no'. The most important aspect of a social pedagogue practitioner's work is interventions with his clients. The sociologist analyses and interprets. He uses theory to try to interpret processes and tendencies in groups and in society (Garsjø, 2001). The practising social pedagogue has a stronger orientation towards individuals, and as far as groups are concerned, he is mainly interested in what the sociologist would call small groups, for example, families. However, whereas the social pedagogue's knowledge has one leg firmly planted in psychology, it has another equally firmly planted in sociology. The terms 'normality' and 'deviation' again pop up as useful tools for the social pedagogue, and by adopting a perspective oriented towards sociology, he will be able to find a different understanding to the one he gets when adopting a psychological perspective. A sociological perspective on normality and deviation is less to do with feelings and cognition, and more to do with the mechanisms that include and exclude individuals and groups in society. This gives him a view on the social forces that define what people and groups do. He may also identify structural forces – which, in this context, can be understood as the assertion of power – and other power relations. The theory that the practising social pedagogue gets from sociology will help him to help his client find his place in society as a whole.

We should also mention that some social pedagogic theorists are clearly oriented towards sociology, as, for example, Hegstrup (2007) claims that Madsen (2006) is. Historically, however, social pedagogic theory is solidly grounded in pedagogy, as I have previously mentioned with reference to Mathiesen (2008).

Is the social pedagogue a researcher?

In a way, this question was answered in the previous two sections. The practising social pedagogue is not primarily a researcher; he is, first and foremost, a practitioner who works with people. But the proximity of social pedagogy to psychology and sociology invite us to look at the relationship these professions have to research. Both are disciplines with research at their centre. A lot of psychological research is based on a natural science tradition, while the research base in sociology is found in social science. This is worth noting. What social pedagogy has in common with psychology is the work to improve the situation for concrete individuals. But its most obvious research tradition is the same as that of sociology.

Let us see if we can find traces of research in what a social pedagogue does. In other words: how are social pedagogic methods related to research methods? In this book, I am making the point that an important aspect of social pedagogic work is that it is both ordinary and systematic. The systematic aspect points in the direction of certain tasks and ideals that look like those of a researcher. Before doing anything, the social pedagogue needs to investigate. Social pedagogic practice rests on an examination of the background and current situation of individual clients. Social pedagogy is a holistic practice, which implies a duty to investigate situations thoroughly. When the social pedagogue has made his investigations, he has to analyse the material he has found. Both these tasks are close to Kvale's (1997, p 21) description of what the qualitative researcher does: 'collecting descriptions of the interviewee's world, with a view to interpreting the phenomena described'. But then the tasks of the researcher and the social pedagogue part company. The next step for the researcher is to discuss various viewpoints and tendencies in his material. He may also present recommendations and conclusions. But, as a rule, it is up to others to implement them. The discussion task is different for the social pedagogue. For him, it is about starting the journey at the practical level. His discussion is not on a theoretical level, but an action-oriented – in other words, practising – level. The researcher always formulates his argument in writing, whereas the social pedagogue often (only) expresses his in thoughts and speech. For the social pedagogue, the argument implies looking at the various possible actions and interventions indicated by investigation and analysis. He is not interested in such actions or interventions as theoretical alternatives. He wants to choose the alternative that seems best for his client, and then use it. His 'interest in research' is closely linked to concrete social pedagogic practice. Only when he carries out an intervention does the preceding intervention have a value. So, for the practising social pedagogue, the investigation has no value in itself, but it is vital as a part of the practice of social pedagogy.

The social pedagogue is also linked to academia in another way. Social pedagogy is a specialist perspective that is developed through research. Understanding and methods develop in interaction between the practical and the theoretical field. I have said it before: social pedagogic practice must be informed. This is dependent on a link to academia.

Is the social pedagogue a philosopher?

Like the philosopher, the social pedagogue is interested in understanding, in grasping what is behind the obvious. But there is a big difference between the philosopher and the social pedagogue. The philosopher is normally mostly interested in general and broad questions. To the extent that he focuses on the individual, it is as a *concept* rather than as a person. The social pedagogue focuses on the individual as a person, both on his own and as a member of a group, and his interest is in *the practical application of* the understanding he seeks.

I would also like to link the topic of ethics to the question of the social pedagogue and philosophy. Ethics and morality are and must be closely connected to the work of the social pedagogue. Ethical and moral standards are used to measure what is the right social pedagogic intervention. However, ethics, as used by social pedagogy, does not only concern philosophy. It is closely linked to each individual the social pedagogue works with, the situation the person finds himself in and the actual interventions that the social pedagogue instigates (or chooses *not* to instigate). Social pedagogic ethics are, thus, linked to both philosophy – to general considerations about what constitutes the right intervention – and to the social pedagogue's actual practice in the work with individual clients.

Is the social pedagogue a politician?

Both yes and no. Let us start with the latter. The social pedagogue is not a politician in the sense of shaping policy. He does not work on an ideological level. The task of a politician is to chart a course for where we are heading, and to prepare the ground so that we can go that way. Political ideas belong in the world of visions, but some of the policies adopted have a direct impact on the work of the social pedagogue. Politicians may, for example, pass new laws regulating child welfare, in which case, it becomes the task of the social pedagogue to put them into practice. When politicians decided that child welfare services should concentrate their efforts more on home-based measures, as they did in Norway in 2001,[1] it had direct consequences for how individual child welfare workers had to carry out their jobs. So, in a way, the social pedagogue does work in close conjunction with the politician. We could say that the social pedagogue is a practitioner of policy.

Social pedagogic interventions are often closely linked to political decisions, and also, therefore, to political ideas. Sometimes, this is more obvious than others. Let us take a look at preventive work. Preventive work with young people has had different conditions in different periods and in different parts of the country. Sometimes, the politicians have gone in for youth clubs and outreach work. In other periods, this work has been given a low priority. When politicians decide to go in for preventive work, as a rule, it is social pedagogues (and other professionals) who are brought in to carry it out. That is because the political ideas about prevention fit in with social pedagogic priorities for young people. If the politicians, in turn, decide to give less priority to, for example, outreach services in a town, the social pedagogues are put to the test. Will they accept the political provisions and find other tasks in other contexts? Or will they protest on behalf of the professional ideas they believe in and the young people who are affected by the changed priorities? Up to a certain point, social pedagogues can choose to what extent they want to accept political regulations or to oppose them. Regardless of what they choose, it could be interpreted as *both* a political and professional choice.

I said earlier that the social pedagogue does not shape policy. Now, let me challenge this statement. Through his work with individuals and groups, the social pedagogue acquires knowledge of life conditions and how his clients handle theirs. Freire (1990) is particularly interested in linking the work with vulnerable people to a political understanding. Freire regards pedagogy as a field of work that needs to be deployed in order to give people dignified lives. He advocates a liberating action theory, and claims that 'in the theory of dialogical action, subjects cooperate in order to change lives' (Freire, 1990, p 157). Social pedagogic effort in the practice field is significant also for the politician – politicians are not untouched by what the social pedagogue does. Politicians often take inspiration from encounters with the social pedagogic practice field. In such cases, descriptions given by the social pedagogue will have a direct influence on policy. Eriksson (2005, p 63) touches on something similar when she states that 'politics develop society "from the outside" and pedagogy "from the inside"'. According to Langager and Vonslid (2007, p 3), there is broad agreement about one aspect of social pedagogy: namely, that the definition of what are regarded as social and individual problems 'is extremely sensitive to the economic situation'. Social pedagogy is strongly linked to politics and to the conditions at any time in the society where it is practised.

Is the social pedagogue an advocate?[2]

This question is posed in the context of actual social pedagogic practice. Working with his clients, the social pedagogue often comes across people who need help to formulate their wishes, satisfy their needs and find people and institutions that may be able to help. These are central tasks for the social pedagogue. Advocates represent their clients. Social pedagogues may do the same, in parallel with what Payne (1991) claims is an important aspect of social work. They can help their clients put their case, for example, to the municipal social welfare board. From time to time, they may even be able to fight a case for their clients, perhaps against unreasonable treatment or injustice from officialdom. There is still a significant difference in the way advocates and social pedagogues work. As a rule, the advocate represents his client and does a job *for* him. This is not enough for the social pedagogue. For him, the right thing is to do a job *together with* the client. My understanding of social pedagogic practice tells me that being solely a spokesperson for the client is wrong. The social pedagogue gladly accepts the task of helping people in difficult situations, but he will always have another aim: namely, that the client should be helped to help himself, to learn something about solving the type of problem that they are working on together. This is one difference between the social pedagogue and the advocate. Rather than taking him by the hand and pleading his case at the social security office, the social pedagogue works on preparing his client in how to deal with this encounter. One of the most important aims of this method is for the client to be able to do it without the help of the social pedagogue next time. Another issue is that, from time to time, the social pedagogue has to contradict his client if that is required. It may be that the client needs to be compelled to reflect on his own negative choices, for example, to get a handle on drug abuse. An alternative task may be putting pressure on a client, who has got stuck in a 'more-of-the-same' way of thinking, to adopt an alternative approach; in which case, it can be important to contradict and challenge him.

There is also an important difference between the advocate and the social pedagogue on a theoretical level. In the main, the former has one theoretical source, namely, the law. The latter has many, where the law represents but one of the theoretical perspectives that, from time to time, are 'borrowed'.

We get another understanding of the term 'advocate' by saying that an advocate is also a spokesperson. He is someone who talks about general problems and needs in a group of people – or, for that matter, in individuals. These may be groups that have been 'forgotten' by society, or who are marginalised. This role of spokesperson could be said to be inherent in the social pedagogue's understanding of his profession. The ethical foundation document for the professions of child welfare pedagogues, social workers and social educators (FO, 2002, p 6) states that 'the primary loyalty shall be to the most vulnerable party' when this ends up in conflict situations with, for example, the authorities. The foundation document also emphasises the responsibility to inform others when discovering 'circumstances which create social problems and contribute to social exclusion or undignified life conditions' (FO, 2002, p 10).

Is the social pedagogue an entrepreneur?

In the last few pages, I have been comparing the professional practice of the social pedagogue to that of other professional groups – both as far as their actions, and the knowledge base from where their actions stem, are concerned. My last question in this comparison exercise is a hint that I am also looking for something else. Here, the social pedagogue's professional practice is linked to what we could call a function, namely, the function of creating something new, or initiating something. In social pedagogic practice oriented towards social constructionism, the innovative element has a special place. The social pedagogue is not satisfied with merely meeting the client's needs; he will not be satisfied until the client can meet his own needs. It is, therefore, important to him to uncover something in the client's life that can be used as a springboard to help him move forward (Storø, 2001). So, the social pedagogue does not create opportunities from nothing, he builds on the client's own contribution. Here, we see a parallel meaning of entrepreneur – which (in Norwegian) can refer to someone who *coordinates a major building project*. Thus, entrepreneurship can imply both innovation and the coordination of existing resources.

I have tried to show that the social pedagogue's work involves using elements from several other professional fields. The social pedagogue needs a compound competence. That is part of who he is. He also needs to be able to put the compound together in a different way to the professional groups from whom he gathers knowledge, learning and inspiration. Hämäläinen (2005, p 31) argues that social pedagogy should not be 'reduced to a discipline for and about one specific profession, but rather developed as a science for all who work with people's need for social safety, integration and participation in society, as fellow citizens'. Another important aspect of the role is that the social pedagogue practitioner must both *want* and *dare* to be a professional, that is, to stand up for his social pedagogic expertise. In a practice field whose identity partly stems from activities also found in other professions (as I have shown), it becomes particularly important to try to find the essence of one's own field. Besides, it is in everyday life that a social pedagogue carries out much of his work, in what I call ordinary, everyday situations. Many people know something about bringing up children and young people, and this forces the social pedagogue to clarify his particular competence.

The practitioner makes use of three different types of competence. Skau (2005) suggests three divisions of professional competence: personal competence; theoretical knowledge; and field-related skills. My discussion in this book is primarily based on the last two of these; however, we also need to devote some space to personal competence. In the next chapter, I will discuss the different aspects of personal competence. But let us first round off the part that most clearly deals with theoretical knowledge and field-related skills. When juxtaposed, these concepts help us to look at the relationship between theory and practice, and, as such, they underpin the main message in this book. As I see it, these two interact in a way that captures much of what I understand as central to the practising, practice-oriented social pedagogue: the importance of developing skills, both when it comes to analysis and practice. The picture we get is of a very complex professional field: the social pedagogue as researcher and philosopher, whose practice shares the characteristics of social work, teaching, maybe even the law, and with everything done in the spirit of the entrepreneur.

Personal competence

Many job adverts seeking people for positions with a social pedagogic orientation emphasise the importance of personal suitability. This notion is rarely explained. Being suited to a job implies having both personal and specific professional qualifications. Personal suitability can be understood as an element in what Skau (2005) calls personal competence. This is often understood as *using oneself as a person* when performing professional interventions. Skau (2005, p 59) describes it as 'a unique combination of human qualities, characteristics and skills which we adjust and use in our work-related contexts'. She also points out that this particular type of competence is vital in order to be able to reach our targets with theoretical knowledge and specific professional skills.

The first answer to the question of what constitutes personal suitability must be that the *person* who has the job is very important in these professions. The personal factor is maybe more important here than in many other professions, because the work is done through relationships between people that are being played out in ordinary, everyday situations. Some of the personal aspects required in other professions are also important for social pedagogues. Roughly speaking, we can divide these into two different categories: what any serious employer demands from his employees; *and* what serious employers in the social pedagogic field demand. The first usually involves the qualities that are generally expected of employees, such as reliability, loyalty, specialist knowledge, willingness to work hard, being organised and so on. These are, of course, also important in social pedagogy-oriented jobs. Maybe they are even particularly important in such jobs, as the social pedagogue is also a model for his clients. You cannot work in an institution for young people and skive off work, or in child welfare services without loyalty to the fundamental idea of child welfare. Such social pedagogues would lack credibility. The other side of the notion of personal suitability is linked to the actual content of social pedagogic practice. My perspective is that the social pedagogue *is* his own most important tool. In which case, it is not unreasonable to subject *the person* who carries out the work to certain requirements, linked to the professional ideals for such work. Different workplaces will have different priorities in this respect.

As I have mentioned earlier, informed practice can be linked to reflection. Mathiesen (1999, p 67) ascertains that 'a professional care worker ought to have the competency of reflecting in advance of acting in order to be able to act in an ethically correct way'. For his part, Schön (2001) is interested in 'reflection-in-action'. Both these competencies are important in their own way. So, we can talk about general professional competence – that of a practising social pedagogue. However, this competence is not like that of a craftsman. Whereas the bricklayer learns to build a brick wall that is perpendicular to another and the carpenter learns to build a house with level floors, the social pedagogue learns to a far lesser degree exactly *what* he should be doing. He is, therefore, dependent on something else to guide his practice. I will call this a professional attitude. In this context, the professional attitude of a social pedagogue is, first and foremost, utilising his ability to reflect. The two are closely connected. We could say that this competence also has to do with whether one has acquired a reflective attitude. Røkenes and Hansen (2006, p 75) recommend 'enabling continuous professional reflection', which provides the opportunity to change 'one's way of thinking and one's emotional and behavioural reaction patterns'. Through the reflection process, all aspects of the practice can be put under the microscope, so this is an important tool for critically investigating one's own work. Sævi (2007, p 117) is particularly insistent that the pedagogue 'in an interpretative way [reflects] on who he is and what his actions mean to the child'. This, she says, is because it is through reflection that we can begin to fulfil the intention that the pedagogic relationship is in the child's best interest. Parton and O'Byrne (2000) claim that reflection is the function that leads to the ability to change. It is important to the social pedagogue, but also to the client. By inviting the client to reflect with him, the social pedagogue can help the client to acquire reflective competence. This can also be translated to development competence.

Let us look at some suggestions for the kind of social pedagogic content that we might want to include in the concept of personal competence. I will use Larsen (2004) as a starting point. He has summarised what Kreuger (1986a, 1986b) thinks about this, and added his own viewpoints.[3]

Kreuger thinks that those who work with children and young people must:

- be genuinely interested in children and young people (communicated through both actions and behaviour);
- understand that it takes time to develop a good relationship;
- be ready to discuss personal values and attitudes;
- be able to compromise, but also be authoritative when required;
- be able to observe, analyse and plan;
- have a sense of fun and a good dose of humour – but never be sarcastic;
- be patient and able to welcome small changes;
- be curious, keen to get to know every individual; and
- have his basic needs covered outside the job.

To sum up, the social pedagogue needs to be:

- flexible, but not indulgent;
- sensitive, but keeping a professional distance;
- authoritative, but not oppressive; and
- energetic and optimistic.

I shall not comment in detail on each and every one of Kreuger's points. Most of them speak for themselves. My understanding of what is important here is that the practising social pedagogue must have one view directed towards his client, and another directed towards himself. The former implies openness towards the other person and a basic belief that he is significant. The latter concerns the social pedagogue's ability to observe himself and to work on his own attitudes. These are very important points. I would also like to expand a little on Kreuger. I imagine that the social pedagogue described here could easily be a soft and fairly flexible person. We need to ask ourselves whether his 'adultness' could disappear, or at least become blurred. Dale (2006) and Manger (2005) show that adult authority is under pressure these days. This is particularly problematic during upbringing, because an adult who leaves authority behind loses credibility. Kreuger mentions the need for authority, but it only merits a subordinate clause and lacks clarity.

This could cloud the issue. The authoritative role of the adult must be thematised; if not, we risk that it becomes taken for granted – or forgotten. Henggeler et al (2000) distinguish between an authoritarian and authoritative style of upbringing. The former is characterised by parents showing a high degree of control and little warmth towards their children. An authoritative style of upbringing, on the other hand, is described as parents being attentive to the children's own formulation of their needs and wishes, at the same time as having age- and development-related expectations of them. A description of personal suitability ought, therefore, to define *using professional authority in a balanced way* as an important criterion for personal competence. Showing authority without being authoritarian is a very important component in the practising social pedagogue's work. I have touched on it elsewhere in this book; the client has got to be able to expect the social pedagogue to use all the tools he has got. The authority inherent in the social pedagogue's knowledge and experience is exactly what the clients want. If they could have managed without it, they would never have become clients. At the same time, it is important to understand that specialist knowledge and competence gives the social pedagogue the upper hand. The authority must be used in a way that it is in the client's interest. It must never serve other interests than what is best for the person needing help. This provision is parallel to child welfare legislation about *the child's best interest.*

I would also like to add that the social pedagogue must have the ability to be realistic. This counterbalances some of what is important to Kreuger. He pats us on the head and tells us to be optimistic in the work with our clients. Whereas it *is* important to be optimistic for the people we work with, we have to guard against daydreaming on their behalf. Being realistic implies that the social pedagogue must be able to see what is possible to change, and, not least, what is *not* possible – or advisable – to change. It is easy to be caught in the professional trap of trying to achieve a bit more than what is realistic. Good social pedagogic work, therefore, takes a serious look at the possibilities *and* considers the limitations. The latter is occasionally forgotten in the everyday working life of the practising social pedagogue. I raise this important point under the heading of personal suitability because it would be problematic if a professional's personal score on the optimism–pessimism scale were decisive. The fundamentally optimistic person who trains to become a social pedagogue may end up in a situation where he cannot see any limitations. Limitations may lie with the client, with the social pedagogue himself or in the context of the situation. A common trap that practising social pedagogues are caught in is endless optimism and a positive belief that 'everything is possible', forgetting that the world of the client is not always as simple as they might wish. The professional who thinks optimistically along the lines of 'you can never be positive enough' would probably get support from his employer, from politicians, clients' families and others who happen to be involved. There is something almost unassailable about optimism. The person who tries to bring in some realism can easily come to be regarded as someone who destroys the focus on opportunities, in which case, there is a problem with understanding the relationship between these two concepts. However, one does not exclude the other. On the contrary, they are as closely linked as two sides of the same coin.

The far too optimistic professional actually risks committing an injustice towards his client by forgetting to focus on the difficult road ahead for the person who is actually going to walk it. One of his tasks is to help his client when the going gets tough.

The concepts of 'optimism' and 'pessimism' have a parallel in the concepts of 'opportunity' and 'limitation'. As a starting point, let us use a conversation between Stein, aged 14, who is a member of a youth club, and the social pedagogue, Anne, who works at the club:

> As Anne enters the big common room at the club she spots Stein sitting alone and staring into space. She is used to Stein being actively engaged in what is going on and hanging out with the others. Anne is very observant, and therefore notices the boy's unusual behaviour. Anne goes up to Stein and asks how he is. Stein sighs heavily and says that he is dreading going home that evening and telling his parents about the serious conversation he has had with his teacher today. The teacher has told him that he is in danger of failing two important subjects. Anne asks Stein how he is planning to raise this with his parents. Stein says that he doesn't know what to say, and that he is worried about it. He says that he expects them to get very angry, and that it will be no use talking to them. Anne offers to talk to him about what he might do.

Let us have a look at some possible opportunities that may arise from Anne's conversation with Stein. She would like to help him with what he finds difficult, but she knows that he will have to have the conversation with his parents himself. By focusing on opportunities, she is helping Stein to consider whether he can find something to hang on to in a situation where he only sees problems. Anne is hoping that he will be able to go beyond his comfort zone and do something new. At the same time, she needs to be realistic. It is by no means certain that Stein will be able to do what she suggests. In other words, Anne must work in an uncertain 'landscape' where she does not know the result of her intervention. Maybe every social pedagogic conversation swings between ideal and reality in this way. If so, the social pedagogue needs to be able to plan both for what he expects to happen and for the unexpected. An important social pedagogic competency is, therefore, to be able to work towards a goal, and then turn around and do something else if a change of tactics proves necessary.

Larsen (1994) has a few suggestions for additions to Kreuger's list of what we might understand as personal suitability in the work with children and young people. His suggestions can be summed up in the following five points:

- Being a good role model both in terms of skills and attitude.
- Being able to tolerate provocation (here, understood as the children's or the young people's chaotic and painful inner world) without taking it personally.

- Having a well-developed ability to communicate in a decentred way (taking the young people's perspective *and*, at the same time, keeping one's own).
- Being able to see conflict as a resource.
- Showing sensitivity in the meeting with children and young people.

The fourth point, in particular, needs some explanation. Conflict is normally viewed as something negative, whereas Larsen suggests regarding it as a resource. This is a central point in social pedagogic practice, and I will return to it in a more general context in Chapter Seven.

Totalling all these elements that describe what is meant by personal competence can make anyone feel inadequate. Who on earth would be able to fulfil all these requirements and, at the same time, be themselves? And this is important; staying true to oneself while striving to acquire good professional attitudes and learning to act on the basis of them. Many clients are interested in things totally different from *decentred communication* or *analytically oriented* social pedagogues. If you ask them, what they often want is to be well treated. To be *seen* as a human being; that someone should bother to listen to them. In addition, they are often keen that the social pedagogue should show a little of himself. There is no contradiction in what was said earlier and what I mention here. Both Kreuger and Larsen express the constant requirement of treating people 'properly'. This standpoint is expressed in specialist language; and, furthermore, they list certain professional practice requirements of social pedagogues, in addition to their 'being human'. Later, I will discuss some elements that may merit closer inspection beyond what is suggested by Kreuger and Larsen, including some new suggestions.

Both these authors are interested in roles and tasks that may appear contradictory. As such, they capture the diversity in social pedagogic practice. One point they both make is that the social pedagogue must be able to be an authority/model, at the same time as being open to the child's perspective. Occasionally, you meet social pedagogues who only care about one side of this duality, either because they have failed to understand the importance of taking in the child's perspective, or because they think it is wrong to exert adult authority. Maybe this stems from individual, deep-rooted preferences. People choose to work in the caring professions for very different reasons. Such reasons and one's own personal history often colour people's understanding of what makes a good social pedagogue. Working to become a good social pedagogue practitioner also implies working with oneself. We could call this *working on personal–professional development*. Neither Kreuger nor Larsen expresses this clearly enough. It is hinted at, but not explicitly stated. Their concepts of personal competence may seem a little rigid; it *can* be interpreted as if they are expressing desirable *characteristics* in people who want to work with children and young people. If so, this cannot be right. The first task of the person working with children and young people is not to acquire certain characteristics. He needs to work on his own attitudes and his own skills in such a way that he develops in the direction of these ideals. It will always be problematic to think of these ideals as characteristics. This lacks a certain dynamism. Characteristics may be seen as something you either have or you do not have. It is more dynamic to think of personal suitability as a process. We ought, therefore, to extend the list of personal competencies to include *willingness and ability to work on one's own development, both personal and professional.*

The person who wants to work on his own development will benefit from clearly expressing his attitude, both to himself and to colleagues. This can be done in dialogue with colleagues and worked on in various supervisory sessions. At the same time, it involves looking for professional development, undergoing further training and participating in seminars. It also involves reading new professional literature; keeping an eye on the development of the profession. So, a good attitude is not enough; we can also say that, in this case, *it is about what you do.* The last point may not always be obvious in the social pedagogic field. *That* is a paradox. Most of us would rather not step on a plane where the pilots had not closely followed the very latest technical literature in their field. It is not just the pilot who takes the life of others in his hands. The social pedagogue does too, even if it is in a very different way.

Kreuger and Larsen's suggestions for how to understand personal competence are linked to the core situation in the social pedagogue practitioner's work: meeting the client. I think it is also important to have a look at other situations that the social pedagogue finds himself in. He works in many places where the client is *not* present. One such place is the collegial group. Another is in meetings with his cooperation partner. A third is administrative tasks, for example, budget work for the place where he practises his profession. Larsen's (2004) concept of primary and secondary tasks can help us to expand the concept of personal competence. The direct meeting with the client is a primary task. When the social pedagogue is working in a place where the client is not physically present, he is usually engaged in secondary tasks. These tasks also require descriptions of criteria for personal suitability. I mentioned earlier that the social pedagogue's knowledge base spans several professions. This ought to be reflected in cooperation with others. The social pedagogue cooperates with his closest colleagues, and also with professionals from other bodies. Interdisciplinary work is often referred to as an ideal these days. I would suggest that it is a mark of social competence when the social pedagogue actively chooses to collaborate with others – and works at improving the collaboration. This requires an understanding of the value of such collaboration. Thus, we find an important element of personal competence in working with secondary tasks: the professional in collaboration with other professionals.

Notes
[1] Parliamentary report no. 40–2001/02.

[2] In Norwegian, the word *advokat* has two meanings: the first is a legal representative; and the second is a spokesperson in a general sense.

[3] Neither Kreuger nor Larsen writes explicitly about the social pedagogue; rather, they write about professional groups who work with children and young people. I am responsible for using their material to say something about social pedagogues. I presume that neither of them would have a particular problem with regarding their material in this context.

CHAPTER FIVE

What does the social pedagogue do?

The social pedagogue works with people, with children and young people in various situations, who have different problems with which they, for some reason, need help. The problems may be of a personal kind for some, or they may be problems in the family. In addition, the social pedagogue works with problems linked to the relationship of an individual or a group to his local environment or with society. The social pedagogue works on individual, group and societal levels.

In this chapter, I am going to discuss some concepts that I regard as fundamental in social pedagogic practice. I shall describe them separately, but note that they are only meaningful when considered together. The three concepts are relationships, structure and change. The concepts are not to be understood as complementary or as different phenomena without an internal connection. I shall describe each in turn, because, at first, they appear separate and they will therefore be easier to understand like that. They then have to be fitted together to form a bigger picture, which will help us get to grips with understanding social pedagogic practice. Through this, I will describe what I have chosen to call the social pedagogic context.

Relationships

Working with people means entering into some kind of relationship with them. How this relationship is understood varies from workplace to workplace. This variation is often linked to local traditions, and these are, again, linked to the theoretical perspective on the work. The reason is that different orientations do not value the significance of relationships in the same way. Nevertheless, one general perspective is very often common to all. Røkenes and Hansen (2002, p 21) conclude that what they call supporting relationships, are important in order to support 'the professional's most important task ... to behave in such a way that he or she promotes learning, development, consciousness-raising, liberation, growth, mastering, or better functioning in the other person'.

A lot of the specialist literature about relationships has been developed on a common foundation. It treats relationships as an element in the work towards change, without stopping to think about who the client is. Is this reasonable? Are relationships the same when we work with a man or a woman? With someone old or young? Or with a native citizen versus an immigrant? Many would claim that relationships built on voluntariness and active choices can be different to those that are forced. It is, therefore, useful to investigate what such circumstances can lead to for the relationship, for example, by investigating the client's motivation for entering into a relationship with his helper (Storø, 2001). According to Skau

(2003), the relationship between client and helper is ambiguous. She focuses, in particular, on the tension between the positive in the help that is given and the opportunities for abuse of power that lie in the professional position. If we regard the relationship in a constructionist perspective, we will need to take into consideration that there are many ways to understand relationships. It is the people who participate in a relationship who construct what it consists of. In such cases, factors like gender, age and ethnicity will play a part. People's understanding of the reality they construct with others is shaped by their social experiences. Helgeland (2007) provides an example of how clients construct different understandings of relationships according to the gender they represent. In her study, the male former clients said that they had found relationships with girlfriends or cohabiting partners and their family useful when starting the hard work of building a dignified life. Women interviewees put an equal emphasis on becoming a mother. The men in this study pointed out that support from a partner worked for them, while the women emphasised the adoption of a caring responsibility.

Clients regard the contact with a professional as an important aspect of personal change. According to Howe (1993), the general picture given by research into the client position is that clients do not regard the treatment as the most important factor for change. They consider it much more important that the professional talks, understands and accepts the client.

Professional relationships are different from other relationships, though they do, of course, contain some of the same elements. For example, honesty would be positive and lies negative both in professional and other relationships. In the same way, giving something back to the other person will most often have a positive effect in both types of relationship. But the professional relationship always has another purpose than the private. While the private relationship, on the whole, exists in its own right, professional relationships come about because one person needs help from another. Besides, this help is given in exchange for the professional's salary (Nerdrum, 1997). Therefore, when it comes to the question of symmetry, this relationship looks different. Aamodt (1997) points out that professional relationships have traditionally been asymmetric. She explains this type of relationship in terms of the helper alone having responsibility for the relationship, while the client's contribution is seen as less important. A more symmetrical relationship implies valuing the client's contribution to such an extent that we can talk about an interactive process. At the same time, Aamodt (1997) warns against too much equality in the relationship between helper and client. The professional relationship requires a different expectation of the degree of equality than the private. An example that illustrates this is that confidences in professional relationships are, in principle, one-way, while, as a rule, they are expected to be mutual in private relationships. In other words, professional relationships are not reciprocal, but one-sided (Sævi, 2007). This means that one person lays down the terms that the other, at least to a degree, must accept. It is important not to forget that mutual consideration, like treating the other person with respect and fairness, also ought to be a part of professional relationships, in both directions. The relationship between parents and a young child is clearly asymmetric. The relationship between the same parents and the same child a few years later when the child is nearly an adult and is moving out does not have the same clear asymmetry. While growing up, the child will experience growing into a more equal position in the relationship with parents.

What does the professional relationship actually consist of? Nerdrum (1997) warns against what I will call romanticising 'the good relationship'. He writes that many people seem to imagine 'a good relationship to be curative in itself' (Nerdrum, 1997, p 74). He therefore recommends that we focus on giving both the helper and the client tasks within the relationship. Using the concept of 'work alliance', we can talk about cooperation and the sharing of tasks between the two (Storø, 2001). There is a parallel here with Larsen's (2004) description of the differing tasks of the milieu therapist and the child/young person.

My understanding of the social pedagogue's relationship to the client is close to what Sævi (2007) calls the pedagogic relationship. She describes it as different from other relationships, and goes on to say that it is 'an indissoluble practical-moral unit encompassing the child's holistic learning and development and the adult's upbringing and teaching' (Sævi, 2007, p 107). The purpose of this relationship is 'simply to help the child to grow up' (Langeveld, 1975, recounted in Sævi, 2007). In this way of thinking about relationships, we see that the pedagogic element is the very reason for the relationship and that which gives it content and direction. Having said that, Sævi's description puts more emphasis on the teaching element than I would assume to be natural for the *social* pedagogue's relationship. At the same time, it is also clear that everyday situations contain clear elements of teaching. However, I consider it more important to emphasise some of the other elements in her account. She claims that the adult's pedagogic intention is what creates the opportunity to act pedagogically. How the adult (the social pedagogue) sees the child is therefore vital. Sævi (2007, p 119) puts it like this: 'Being seen pedagogically is being recognised by the adult both as the person you are, and as the one you have not yet become, but can become'. Here lies an understanding that includes both the individual as he constructs himself now, and the individual's possible construction of himself in the future. This striving is recognised in the relationship, and it is through the relationship that the adult offers his participation in the constructions.

Relationships have both a concrete and a more hidden side. They are concrete in the sense that, as a rule, the people in a relationship have something to say about it. For example, you could say: 'I know a man'. Often, you can also say something about the various qualities of the relationship: 'He's always there for me when I need him'. As a rule, people know when they have a relationship with someone. But, at the same time, they only know part of what characterises the relationship. Levin (2004) suggests thinking about each relationship as two relationships: my relationship to you and your relationship to me. This includes the assumption that each person can only know one side of the relationship. The other side is basically unknown to us. Of course, the other person can tell us about it. If a person says 'I love you', the other knows something about the first person's side of the relationship; but still only a small part. Some of the other person's picture will always stay hidden from us.

What I call the hidden side of relationships is to do with the fact that relationships include a lot of things that are unspoken. It is possible to agree on a relationship to some extent, but not fully. You could, for example, say 'Let's be friends'. But there is still a lot in the relationship that is hidden, outside the rational and agreed – and also outside what can be spoken of in concrete terms. What I call the hidden side has to do with the fact that relationships are, to a great extent, based on feelings. It is, therefore, only possible, and desirable, to describe relationships through the use of language up to a certain point.

The relationship between the social pedagogue and the client is also influenced by this, though in very different ways. Before expanding on this, I would like to introduce some people I know.

Maja, Monica and Thomas know each other. They are all young people supported by child welfare services. One day, they are talking about the adults from the services. Maja gets the feeling that the other two have a completely different relationship with the adults who are responsible for them than she has. She is surprised by this.

Maja has been placed in foster care. She has experienced a turbulent childhood, but is now living with a foster family where she is doing well. She knows that she can stay there as long as she needs to. She feels like a part of the foster family, and knows that these are people she will consider her own family even when she has grown up.

Her friend Monica lives in a residential home for young people. She will stay there until she is 18. Monica says she is fine at the home, but she is ready to move out as soon as she can make her own decisions. She is in reasonably close touch with her mother and an older brother. These are the people she regards as her family. When Monica describes her relationship to the adults who work at the home, Maja notices that she talks about them in a completely different way to how she would have described her own relationship to her foster parents. Monica says she gets on well with several of the milieu therapists, but she doesn't think that she will have much contact with them after she has moved out; except maybe with one, who has indicated that she might be interested in supporting Monica in her independent life.

The girls have got to know Thomas, and they have told him that they are placed in foster care and in an institution. Thomas tells them that he, too, is in touch with the child welfare services. "But I actually live at home", he says. The child welfare services have employed a social worker for interventions to support his parents at home. Maja and Monica wonder why, and Thomas tells them that it's to do with his involvement in petty crime and neglecting school for many years. "And my dad and I argue quite a lot, and all hell breaks loose", he says. He says that the family has a lot of contact with a milieu therapist, but that he doesn't talk to her a lot himself. The therapist has asked Thomas for his views on the work she is doing in the family, and he knows that she would talk to him if he asks her, but he can't really be bothered with it. Maja thinks that if she were in Thomas's situation, she would probably have missed being in close touch with the person who was supposed to be helping her.

These three young people all have a relationship to the adults who work with them. However, Maja's sense that these relationships are all very different appears to be right. This is probably intended by the people who work with them. Part of the reason will be found in the type of task they have taken on; and part in the theory they have based their work on. Let's meet them.

Kai and Helene are Maja's foster parents. Kai says: "When we first met Maja we quickly decided that we wanted to try to make her feel secure so that she wouldn't have to move again." "For me, this was a question of commitment", Helene continues. "I myself had a very secure upbringing, and I know how much it means. I thought we could offer her something that we felt sure was important to her."

The name of the milieu worker with special responsibility for Monica is Berit. She says that she has known Monica for a year: "In the beginning, I thought it was hard to work with Monica. It was as if she hadn't really moved in with all of herself. I was assigned to follow her up closely and had to find something to do with her. So I invited her to come and stay at a weekend cabin. We went skiing together and, after that, our relationship improved. I have now offered to be her support person when she moves out, and I think she will accept that. I will try not to take on any new milieu contact responsibility during the first period after Monica has moved out. I think this is an important signal to her."

"I normally meet Thomas's family three times a week", says Kristin, who is the home milieu therapist. She has been working with the family for four weeks, and is beginning to know them well enough to initiate the first interventions. "I have talked a lot to the parents, but Thomas himself has kept a distance", she says. "I'm planning to have a chat with him now and then, to see what he thinks about the work his parents and I are doing. I am not particularly worried that he doesn't want to talk to me. I am far more interested in improving the dialogue between Thomas and his father. I hope we have managed to get some way towards solving this when the intervention period has ended and I withdraw from the family."

The adults, who I will call social pedagogues in this context, even if Kai and Helene are not trained as such, give different accounts of 'their' young people. It is also quite clear that the relationships are very different, at least in the way these adults perceive them. The three youngsters also gave three different descriptions.

Let us look more closely at what the social pedagogues had to say about the relationships. Kai and Helene were preoccupied with their own commitment, and Maja needed exactly such a commitment from them. They had given Maja signals about this, and it appears that she had understood this and accepted the offer of a particular type of relationship. The expressed commitment here is an indication that the relationship has been a goal in itself. Kai and Helene had a theory that a relationship of the type they have worked towards would be an important element, maybe even the most important, in their work with Maja.

When Berit talks about working on the relationship with Monica, we get a slightly different picture. She is not talking about a deep and lasting commitment in the same way as we have just witnessed. However, she is interested in a time perspective beyond the here and now, and she is quite clear about her commitment in this respect. The relationship that Berit has developed with Monica is no less important than the one Maja was offered by her foster family, though it is different. As it has more of a time limit, her aim is not the same. You could say that the relationship becomes a means for being able to work with Monica during a critical period of her life. Monica's relational context is more that of a contract than Maja's. Monica clearly knows this, and she accepts it. It may look as if Berit wanted this aspect of the relationship to be openly communicated.

Kristin's relationship with Thomas is quite different from the two we have looked at so far. Some might say that you could hardly call it a relationship. Kristin is not particularly concerned about this. She knows that she is working with some clearly defined goals for change in the parents. One of her main aims is to increase their competence in the upbringing of Thomas. She also understands the importance of herself not becoming too important in the work towards change that the family has to carry out. This is one of the fundamental ideas behind this type of intervention. It is, therefore, not Kristin's aim to achieve anything but a relatively superficial relationship with Thomas. But she finds it useful to talk to him from time to time. She also assumes that it is useful for Thomas to talk to her, at least if he is the one who initiates contact. Therefore, she makes sure that she gets to know him, and makes it clear that there is a possibility they will have some contact in the future. In the short conversations she has had with Thomas, she has talked about the goals of the work she is doing, namely, his criminal behaviour, skiving off school and how they are getting on as a family. For Kristin, the relationship is more of a tool in order to map Thomas's views on the work towards change. In order to discover this, she does establish a relational contact with him, but she thinks about it more as a forum for the work she has to do.

We see that a relationship can be perceived as a goal in itself, as a means of working with the child or young person, or as a forum for developing thoughts and ideas about the work. The first of these relationships has the strongest emotional content; the last has the least of this dimension. The relationship between Berit and Monica is somewhere in between these two as far as emotional involvement is concerned. This type of relationship can both be a means and, at the same time, have similar characteristics to the one Maja was offered.

In these three stories, it appears that the social pedagogues and the young people had reasonably similar perceptions of what kind of relationships the young people needed – and were offered. In conflict situations, this can often be much more difficult.

Monica used to live with a foster family, but this came to an end when she refused to stay there any longer. Monica felt that her foster mother wanted to know 'everything' about her. She also felt that the foster mother did not particularly value Monica's biological mother. Monica was aware that her mother had not always done what she ought to have done, but she had no wish to get a 'new mother'. The result was that Monica moved to a residential home. The foster mother also gradually came to accept that this was the best solution. But she was disappointed that her engagement with Monica had not yielded results. Fortunately, she was offered follow-up help by a wise child welfare worker who explained to her what Monica needed in terms of a relationship, and told her that this was better dealt with in an institution.

When Berit assumed the responsibility for following up Monica at the residential home, the starting-point was that Monica had had a bad relationship experience, in addition to several other similar experiences further back in her relationship history. It was important for Berit to adjust to this, not least by giving Monica time to decide what shape the contact should take.

Relationships are not something you either 'have' or 'do not have'. Relationships are something you can choose to enter into. Or you can choose not to. However, it is also important to understand that this choice is not always a rational one, where one is presented with clear alternatives. We all struggle with our relationships from time to time, whether they are private or professional. We feel that the other person does not understand that a friend, boyfriend or girlfriend does things that do not fit into our own picture of the relationship so far. Or we see that a client suddenly does something that makes us wonder if we have to rethink how to use the relationship in our professional work.

I find it useful to think about relationships as a result of negotiation (Storø, 2001). Thinking about them in this way means that we do not take the relationship for granted. We can see it changing all the time. The relationship is constantly being constructed. Even more precisely, we can say that the relationship(s) is (are) continuously being co-constructed. However, negotiations are just as often non-verbal as verbal. They touch on both open and more concealed elements. As we saw from Berit's account, her relationship with Monica changed in connection with their trip to the weekend cabin. They had a nice time together, and this led to a change in their relationship. By regarding a relationship as something that is negotiable, we also focus on the client's own definition of the relationship. We acknowledge the client's opportunity to decide himself what the relationship should look like. Perhaps being a client, in itself, means making concessions, but we can nevertheless give the client authority over the relationship.

The following are some of the most important factors that influence the social pedagogue's decision about the kind of relationship he should offer individual clients:

- The client's age.
- The client's gender and the social pedagogue's gender.
- The time perspective.
- The theoretical reference framework used.
- The aim of the work (linked to the previous point).
- What kind of other relationships the client has or has access to.
- The client's relational history.

Regardless of the choices we make, there is one general standard. The relationship offered must be credible (Larsen, 2004). 'Credible' implies not promising more than one can deliver – and actually keeping one's promises. It implies being true to what one does, and maintaining a lasting relationship. This credibility can be regarded as the adult stake in the relational game. The child or the young person can choose to receive it, but also the opposite. Genuineness from the social pedagogue increases the possibility of the effort being valued; in which case, the foundation for collaboration will have been laid.

Making oneself available to the client in a relationship capacity can be hard work. Whoever offers themselves to a client in such a role must appreciate that getting personally involved can be difficult. One has to expect being disappointed, and that the disappointment will not be understood by others. In Chapter Four, I touched on Larsen's (1994) particular point about what it takes to be a good social pedagogue. He says that you have to be able to tolerate provocation from a client without taking it personally. In other words, the social pedagogue must attempt not to respond to negative behaviour from the client by 'locking' the relationship or by revenge or punishment. A social pedagogue's specialist knowledge and understanding enables him to perceive such behaviour from the client as based on something other than evil. As Larsen (2004) sees it, they are an expression of the client's painful inner world. When this is on show, it can easily be understood by bystanders as 'acting out'. Having said that, it is, of course, also important that the social pedagogue actually does have a personal reaction, that is, that he reacts 'with himself', with his own emotions. Anything else could easily be seen as mechanistic and robot-like. Only when the contact between client and social pedagogue also contains spontaneity will it be perceived as real. A competent social pedagogue masters both the use of his emotions in the relational interaction with his client and tolerates the client playing out his emotions without this resulting in a doomed relationship between them.

The relationship offers opportunities for empathy towards the one needing help. This is an important aspect for him. However, social pedagogues occasionally misunderstand this empathy task. One of the most common mistakes made by empathy-oriented social pedagogues is almost exclusively trying to meet the basic needs the client has for a significant other. When the helper is brought in, he may immediately see that the client has a difficult relationship history, and maybe also not have much to gain from the relationship offered by the social pedagogue entering the arena. That is hardly surprising if the social pedagogue tries to be the most important immediate person for his client. It *feels good* to be significant for somebody. However, this can be a dangerous choice. He might commit the error of forgetting that this is not exactly what the client needs from the professional. The status of significant other should, first and foremost, arise from relationships that happen by their own force. Only then are they meaningful and real.

The function of the professional relationship is to help this happen, where the goal is for the client to establish good *private* relationships. It is, therefore, only credible when used as a *preliminary* phase with the aim of the client creating good private relationships – which are characterised by another type of credibility. You could say that teaching the client good relationship competence increases his opportunities to be included in various types of communities. In other words, one important hallmark of the professional relationship in social pedagogic practice is that it is temporary. A professional relationship nearly always has a time limit. Some time or other, the client must stop being a client. It *may* then be difficult to meet the expectation that has been created. The social pedagogue makes himself available to give the child or young person some other relationship experiences than the ones he has previously had. Through realising that it is possible to become significant for somebody and possible for someone else to become significant for them, the child or young person will gain new experiences that he can use himself.

The primary goal of the pedagogic relationship is the other person's development as a human being (Sævi, 2007). Its aim should not be to meet basic needs. That belongs in the private sphere. In addition, if we were to clarify the *social pedagogic* reason for the relationship, we would have to add Natorp's statement that man only becomes man through human interaction (recounted in Mathiesen, 1999, p 15). Here, we see an argument for the relational, which points to people's inclusion in society.

Of the social pedagogues we have got to know in these past few pages, only Kai and Helene are considering including some of the hallmarks of a private relationship in their relationship with the young person. They can do this because they are foster parents acting in the place of a parent, and must therefore offer a relationship with clear parallels to a private one.

Structure

The question of structure is an interesting one, though not all social pedagogues appreciate this. For some, this is quite an alien idea. The reason may be that it touches on dimensions that some of the practitioners in this profession regard as problematic. All social pedagogues share an interest in human beings. The concept of relationships is, therefore, a more obvious tool than the concept of structure.

Some regard structure as something inflexible, something that actually hinders social pedagogic practice.

It is, therefore, important to investigate how to understand structure in a social pedagogic context. In a constructionist perspective, we can say that structures are social functions that regulate communities. They are, more or less, expressed social constructions of the culture of a community (cf Burr, 2003). The culture shows itself in the form of expectations, norms and regulations. Negotiated understandings of what is real, what is right and wrong, what is bad and good, find their way into structures. It is through such processes that we arrive at and make decisions based on social assumptions about everyday structural functions, for example, like the human diurnal rhythm. The structure inherent in the adult's opinion that children of a certain age need to go to bed at a certain time is a good example of this. The reasons for such social constructions of structure can be regarded as pedagogic in nature. By putting children to bed at a certain time, we want them to learn about diurnal rhythm. By learning social functions like this, the child gradually becomes included in the human community of active, independent subjects.

In the everyday life of social pedagogy, we often talk about structures, understood as the relevant framework conditions for the practice. As a rule, this concerns outer frameworks provided by budgets, year plans, resources for manpower and the physical working conditions, such as the building design of a particular institution. Understanding structure only as frameworks, and, thus, only as something that limits practice, is too narrow. Structure in social pedagogic practice is *both* outer frameworks *and* inner organisation. Here, by inner organisation, I mean the social pedagogue's own organisation of his work, designed in close contact with other elements of this practice – such as the approach to relationships and ethical considerations. For *some* social pedagogue practitioners, this is the very core of the profession: namely, structured interventions in other people's lives.

During the first meeting of the 'responsibility group', the child welfare worker talks about the importance of a good structure in the foster home. He says that this is just as important to Maja as her feeling that she is welcome. Kai and Helene are a little unsure about this. "Structure? What has that got to do with us?", Kai asks. The child welfare worker explains that the foster home arrangements they are making for Maja will not be credible unless they also work out what kind of diurnal rhythm would suit her, what kind of reactions she should be met with if she breaks the rules and norms in the foster home, and so on. He reminds them that it is not easy to arrive as a new member in an established family and adjust to a system that is taken for granted by those who already live there. Kai and Helene nod thoughtfully at this.

Let us look at what structure really is in a social pedagogic context. Kvaran (1996) links the concept of structure to planning and purpose when he writes about milieu therapy. Systematically organised work processes help us to establish goals for the work, carry out the interventions we think are best and evaluate what we did and the effect it had. Another way to describe structure is that it is closely linked to what Furuholmen and Schanche Andresen (2007) write about when they emphasise the advantage to the client of being able to find predictability and belonging by participating in a social environment with a clear structure in its organisation. When I write about structure in this context, my meaning is close to this understanding. However, Kvaran's understanding is also important in social pedagogic work, something I shall return to later. Let us be even more concrete. I am choosing to understand structure as something that arises from all the choices we make in order to organise the activity of both social pedagogues and clients. According to Garsjø (2003), structure describes a pattern that lasts for a certain period. It is about planning, routines, rules and expressed expectations, norms, roles and tasks. All this helps to regulate communication and collaboration in the environment where the social pedagogue works, for everyone who is there. If we look at this concept in relation to Larsen's (2004) concept of primary and secondary tasks, it will immediately seem that the question of structure belongs in the latter category. It is true that structure often has to do with what needs to be done to solve the primary task. Larsen's definition of the primary task is preparing children and young people for working on their own development and change. Work on developing a structure, for example, in an institution, could be regarded as such preparation. However, the question of structure is sometimes also a direct topic in the relationships and conversations between the child or young person and the social pedagogue.

> Berit spends quite a bit of time with Monica during the first period at the residential home. Some of this is just hanging out together to get to know her, and giving Monica the opportunity to get to know her contact person. Berit also spends time showing Monica all the things you need to know when moving into a new place. Sometimes Monica gets fed up with these conversations and shouts out that all she needs is a place to live! "There is so much to figure out, it's driving me crazy!"
>
> In the second week of living at the institution, Monica does not get back for supper. She is not seen or heard of until she turns up quite late in the evening. She does not answer her phone and does not reply to text messages all evening. Berit decides to use this situation to talk to Monica about why people who work in an institution feel it is important to have certain rules for how to live one's life.

In many ways, institutions are very 'structure-heavy'. Everyone who has lived or worked in an institution knows that it takes a lot of effort to learn and understand all the written and unwritten rules and routines. You need to have the full picture in order to cope well with everyday life in an institution. The question of structure, therefore, becomes particularly pertinent in institutions. Regardless of the choices made by the people who work there about rules and routines, there is a lot to get acquainted with. You need a great deal of organisational understanding to run an institution, but also to live there.

The structure can be understood as an element that keeps order in the everyday lives of the residents of an institution. Some of them lack a good diurnal rhythm, or they live a life without clear social norms to follow. Others may be described as having a chaotic inner world, and need to be surrounded by clear frameworks in order to be able to function well, both emotionally and in terms of behaviour. Professional choices about focusing on the structure and then designing a structure that it is assumed the residents will benefit from is, first and foremost, a choice about *using* the structure. It implies both taking on responsibility for the design of a functional structure and actively using it in everyday life. Larsen (2004) invites us to have a look at structure as a psychological function, writing that a good external structure contributes to the development of the child or young person's inner structure. A more typical social pedagogic perspective would focus more on the potential for learning and formation inherent in having to live for some time in a social context where the structure imposes a challenge to learning. When faced with the structure of an institution, the children or young people will either adjust to it or not. They will either open up about their problems or they will not. We could say that the task of the structure is to help the children or young people to show what they can do (which, at the same time, implies showing what they *cannot* do), and, thus, help them in their development work (Larsen, 1992; Storø, 2005). The institution can be perceived as 'a small world' in the midst of 'the big, wide world'. A world where it is safe to demonstrate what you can and cannot do. The idea is for those who live in the institution to learn something about themselves in relation to a (particular) structure. Then, in turn, they can learn something about how to manage in the world outside the institution, which is, of course, also full of structures.

It is also important to understand structure as something closely linked to relationships. Larsen (2004, p 20) is pointing in this direction when he writes about 'regarding the relationship's structural (organisational) side and the relationship's content as two sides of the same coin'. The content part can, thus, be understood as the qualitative aspect of the relationship, while the structure part can be understood as the regulation of the relationship, in time and space. My own suggestion in terms of understanding the link between relationship and structure is to regard the structure as the room, or the context, where the relationship is played out.

The residents' encounters with the structure become an important arena for learning. But what does a functional structure really consist of? In the spirit of this book, we can, first, say that it needs to have a pedagogic purpose (cf Larsen, 1992, 2004; Storø, 1999, 2001; Sævi, 2007). It must:

- *Be stable, with the ability to change.* We could also say that it needs to be rigid but, at the same time, flexible. This means that the structure represents what is secure and predictable, but also that it has to provide those who live within it with the opportunity for personal development – and, with that, a change in their life conditions.

- *Be clear.* This implies that everyone who is part of a structure ought to be able to get acquainted with its rules and sanctions. It must be easy for them to get a perspective on it so that they can navigate through daily life within the structure without danger.
- *Be designed in the client's best interest.* Institutional structures are no good unless they arise from the needs of the client. One such need, for example, is learning to relate to such a structure, a competency that can be put to good use in society as a whole later in life. The most problematic institutional structures are those designed in the best interest of the staff. An example of this would be timing of supper to suit staff rotas rather than when the clients are hungry. Another requirement is that the structures need to reinforce positive behaviour and progress in the clients.
- *Have space for relational meetings.* The structure can never be separated from the relational aspect of social pedagogic work. The implication of this is that choices made in terms of structure must always support the need for relational meetings between the client and those who work with him. It is, therefore, not sufficient to make decisions – such as about how to organise mealtimes – solely in structural terms. The choices must also take into account how to provide opportunities for dialogue and meetings between those who find themselves within this structure.
- *Be tolerant towards the clients' experimentation.* This implies that clients need a safe environment for their learning processes. In order to learn, they have to try out various alternatives. During this process, they will sometimes succeed, sometimes not. It is by reviewing his experiences through failure and success that the client will learn something new, and the structure needs to accommodate this. In this context, a problematic structure could be described as one that rejects those who fail, in other words, where there is little tolerance for the opposition. Failure will sometimes – at least to untrained eyes – look like *nothing but* provocation, sabotage or opposition.
- *Be subjected to regular evaluation.* Structures tend to become rigid systems rather than flexible aids, and therefore need to be regularly assessed. We could say that structures themselves need a structure for self-evaluation.

Social pedagogic practice is distinctive in that the professional practitioner organises his own practice *as it is happening.* The social pedagogue cannot count on organising his working day by planning for one hour in the morning and then carrying out his plans during the day and summing up the results in the evening. Social pedagogic practice is far too complex for that. Whereas it is often a good thing to plan at the start of a working day and sum up or evaluate when it is over, planning and evaluation must also constantly be happening along the way. In complex practice, the question of structure becomes particularly difficult, simply because it is more difficult to organise what is complex rather than simple.

However, this does not exempt the social pedagogue from including the question of structure in his practice. It is precisely because it is a difficult topic that it needs careful consideration. This means that the social pedagogue must take an interest in organisation and organising, and he must be willing to implement organisational measures in the situation where he and his colleagues meet the client (cf Larsen, 2004).

It is important to point out a structural characteristic of social pedagogic practice: namely, that organisational changes along the way may alter the social pedagogue's own activity in the midst of an interventional phase. This demands a great degree of flexibility and adaptability, greater than in many other professional contexts. If we imagine a dental practice, it is probably possible to define a certain number of tasks and a certain number of interventions that are carried out again and again, week after week.[1] The social pedagogue is less able to work in such a predictable environment. For him, it will just as often be the case that the intervention that brings the solution a step closer is a departure from the planned, from what is already defined. Looking at the acting profession, we can very clearly see the relationship between what is planned and what is not. Most plays are based on a script, where the actor's lines, stage movements and so on are carefully rehearsed in advance. But the actor must also add a personal dimension, an interpretation, which may vary from evening to evening. The interpretation arises from the pre-planned, from the manuscript. Without this, it would not exist. But in his interpretation, the actor is also liberating himself from what is already planned. We see this liberation even more clearly during improvisation. Improvisation is a subtle professional activity that, at its best, contributes to improving professional quality.

Similarly, the social pedagogue must have a plan for his professional activity. Such plans will rarely be so detailed that they can be compared to an actor's script. Rather, they will emerge as predefined images of the planned professional activity in the form of descriptions of what is meant to be happening. We can imagine that the social pedagogue writes down a plan for how he wants to carry out a meeting with a group of clients, and that in this plan, he makes assumptions about what will happen during the various stages of the meeting. During the meeting, he must both stay with his plan and try to carry out as much of it as possible, and be able to depart from it and do something else if the situation demands it.

The structural part of the work is often captured and described in models for understanding the phases of the work and for tasks that need to be systematised. One of the most important arguments in favour of such models is that the client's situation normally is so complex that it is vital to get the best possible overall view of it in order to be able to make the best possible decisions. This requires a structure for the process, which starts with a formulation of the problem, and proceeds via mapping to implementation and then evaluation of interventions (Kvaran, 1996; Grønvold, 1997; Linde and Nordlund, 2006).

One last element, while we are talking about structure, would be to have a look at the structure of the *practice field*. The social pedagogue practitioner is part of a workplace, which, in turn, is part of society's effort to help people who need helping. The professional activity is also determined by theories, knowledge and policy that have been developed elsewhere. These are structural elements in the professional practice.

Change

The social pedagogue's work needs to have a goal. An example of such a goal could be to change something in the lives of people he works with. When the social pedagogue comes into contact with children and young people who have problems in one or several areas, they often already know that they need help from others to solve them. Solving the problems may be the change that is required. The change that social pedagogic practice almost always strives to achieve, however, is that the client acquires increased competence to solve the problem himself. In such cases, the social pedagogue may not even look in the direction of where the problem is. Rather, he will often concentrate on the *client's* problem-solving competence and on possible solutions; in which case, we can say that the social pedagogue is working according to the principle of helping people to help themselves. This way of thinking is found in a solution-focused perspective (Haaland, 2005 {**NIR?**}), which is a fundamental aspect of social pedagogic thinking.

When I write that the work needs to have a goal, it is because there must always be a *reason* to initiate work with people. The reason can be either more or less defined. It can also be either more or less communicated. By that, I mean it can be either more or less clarified for the client. Sometimes, the client knows that he is being exposed to change-oriented work, and other times, not aware of it. Children in nurseries will be less aware of being exposed to social pedagogic change-oriented work than young people living in residential homes because of their behavioural problems. But young people and adults can also be the subjects of change-oriented work without knowing it. It is probably true that young people in youth clubs see themselves as users of an activity centre without realising that those who work there may have goals about, for example, changing attitudes to bullying among youngsters in the part of town where the club is. The parents of a child that has been placed in care may see themselves as cooperation partners when they come to a case conference, while the staff possibly thinks of them more as actors in a process of social pedagogic intervention with the goal of getting the parents to change in order for the child to get more out of the weekends when he is at home. It goes without saying that it would most often be ethically best to be honest and upfront about what we are doing to the people at the receiving end of the work.

I have previously mentioned that social pedagogy is, to a large extent, about what Mathiesen (1999) and Madsen (2006) call pedagogic emergencies. Something 'went wrong' for the child or young person while they were growing up. The social pedagogic task of *bringing up the child* thus becomes a re-upbringing. This includes elements of both repair and construction. When I now bring in the concept of change, it is important to link it to the concept of re-upbringing. It is not the child or the youngster *as a person* that must be changed. Contrary to psychology, which, at least traditionally, has been clearly oriented towards the individual, the social pedagogue's project for change is linked to the child or the young person as a social being. The child or young person's upbringing, their behaviour in social contexts, their values and understanding of themselves as individuals and social actors are possible central areas for the social pedagogue's work towards change. These areas naturally also affect the children/young persons as people, as they are also embedded in the person as a unique set of features that characterises each individual.

Let us bring together our four new acquaintances: Kai, Helene, Berit and Kristin. We meet them as they are having a cup of coffee and talking about similarities and differences in their work. Kristin is talking about a young person for whom she has established clear goals for change, goals that are to be reached in the space of four months.

> Berit asks whether Kristin feels stressed by having to achieve so many changes for Thomas in such a short space of time. She, herself, feels that she does not have enough time to make things happen with Monica, who is moving on next year. "Not really", says Kristin. "There are two things you need to remember: in the kind of change-oriented work that I do, I am concentrating on relatively few goals, and they are very concrete goals. Besides, I am mobilising the whole family. In many ways they have to do the work themselves. I am just 'getting it started'". Helene says that, for them, changing Maja is not a major topic of conversation. "We are trying to create a secure everyday life for her, so that she can develop naturally", she says, and Kai agrees. "I can see parallels to what I am doing in what all three of you are talking about", says Berit. "I probably couldn't have worked in such a concrete way with changing Monica's behaviour as you are describing, Kristin. But, at the same time, I can see that it would not have been enough 'just' to create the conditions for her to develop naturally. It is easier to see that this may be the right thing for you to do for Maja in the foster home."

We can conclude that change is one of the main goals of social pedagogic work. But the three social pedagogues relate to this concept in very different ways. They are also aiming at different things, although we can guess that their long-term goals will be quite similar, namely, that Maja, Monica and Thomas should have good adult lives and that they will be included in constructive communities.

The concept of change needs further investigation. Some of the changes children and young people go through while growing up are natural changes resulting from the maturing process, while others are results of various types of external influences. Larsen (2004, p 21) suggests distinguishing between the concepts of development and change. He writes that 'Development is a "relatively" painless process, while change implies giving something up'. As Larsen writes from a psychological perspective, I understand his concept about development as the mentally healthy and *natural* development that the child or the young person goes through in harmony with their environment. Maturing is a part of this process. He reserves the concept of change for psychologically inexpedient processes that 'need to be worked on so that they can be re-created as developmental processes' (Larsen, 2004, p 21). In Larsen's professional perspective, it is, first and foremost, *the poorly integrated child* who needs processes of change in order to get onto a sound developmental track.[2] Larsen also distinguishes between the work of upbringing and (psychologically grounded) milieu therapy, where the former is regarded as being able to support development processes, while it is possible for the latter to initiate processes of change. He goes on to say that milieu therapy 'also involves upbringing in the sense that it represents a communication of culture and values' (Larsen, 2004, p 89).

This interpretation challenges a social pedagogic way of thinking. Is the social pedagogue only working to support development, or can we regard his efforts as a driver of change? I would like to emphasise that with the concept of 'change-oriented work', I understand both what Larsen chooses to call work that facilitates development and change-oriented work. But then we need to find a concept for change other than the one Larsen is talking about. The social pedagogue is not a psychologist, and his goal should not be to change internal psychological structures. Help comes from the theory of social constructionism. It suggests that we understand the clients' constructions as means of effecting change. Change arises from their work with themselves as participants in social communities. In this context, a construction can be understood as a way to perceive oneself, coupled with how one is seen by others. The assumption here is that when an individual constructs new perceptions of himself, he has changed. He will forever be someone else. The reason we can say that this type of process is not part of the natural, ongoing process that Larsen describes is that it is initiated by someone else. It does not happen by itself, but as a result of the individual, and the community he is part of, changing his story. When, after a while, a person thinks and talks differently about himself through such processes, he *has become* someone else.

Thomas used to get really poor grades at school and his teacher hardly ever said anything positive about his results or his efforts. There was only one subject he mastered quite well, and that was history. He had always enjoyed finding out about the past. But even in this subject, his results were so-so. Thomas had always regarded himself as a loser at school. After a few conversations with Agnes, who was responsible for following him up at school, he made the decision to try to get an A in a history test at least once. For a few weeks, he did a lot of work with Agnes on the subject, and they talked about how Thomas could work on his fear of school tests. When he finally managed to get an A, it was the start of improving his grades in several subjects. When Agnes asked him a few months later what had happened, he replied: "I don't really know. But I do remember that I used to see myself as a real loser here at school, and I don't any more."

Change and processes of change are not real until they can be identified by the person in question. Clients may well change their external behaviour, and this can be a good thing, both for the client himself and for his environment. However, purely external changes will not become a part of the person until they are also seen as useful on an internal level, until the person understands himself differently. The behavioural therapist would say that positive changes in behaviour are maintained when a person experiences external stimuli that reinforce the target behaviour. A social constructionist social pedagogue would be more interested in whether the person has constructed new ways of talking about himself. In particular, it is the story you tell *about yourself, to yourself* that has the potential to effect real change. Pedagogy is, first and foremost, perceived as the adult generation imparting knowledge to children and young people. Larsen (2004, p 89) thinks that 'upbringing has a sharper focus on the child or young person's behaviour as normatively acceptable or unacceptable'. By redefining the pedagogic concept of change, we afford the social pedagogue the opportunity to do something more for the child or young person than simply leading them into the values universe inhabited by adults. *Change, understood as the client's new ways of telling his life story,* can be regarded as a basic concept of social pedagogy.

In this way, we capture the work done by Kai, Helene, Berit and Kristin. But, at the same time, we see that these four put different emphases on development and change – based on the client they are working with and, not least, the context they are working in.

Work towards change in social pedagogic practice can be very diverse, and not only because of the clients' life stories. Focusing solely on this would imply an orientation that is far too individually oriented. A fundamental question in this context is: what is required to make life better for the client? In other words: what is real change? Which brings us to the next question: who decides what is good enough? Some social pedagogues would consider it very important that change must imply better life conditions. It is natural to mention external factors like having a job, going to school (ie meaningful daily activities), a good place to live, adequate income and so on. Others would emphasise the client's social environment, such as relationships, networks and access to social support. A client's life could be significantly changed if he experiences a better understanding of his situation. Processing his understanding of his situation so that it becomes easier to handle could also be a valuable contribution. The latter touches on the linguistic aspect of this practice, which is something I will shortly return to. We should still sound a warning against being overconfident that new ways of seeing this will alter the client's life conditions. For many people, real changes in external, observable conditions are very important. The most important thing of all is to state emphatically that the client himself is the best person to assess whether the change has made a positive difference.

The social pedagogue will always be guided by theory's focus on the inclusion–marginalisation dichotomy when the question of change arises. When he is planning his work on processes for development and change, it is vital to consider whether the client participates in social environments, or whether he is excluded from them in various ways. The client's relationship with the community will always be something that the social pedagogue practitioner needs to assess – and the client's own assessment of this would carry equal weight.

The social pedagogic context

What is the connection between the three concepts of relationship, structure and change? They seem to deal with very different phenomena.

That is precisely it. They do deal with different phenomena, but it is the way these phenomena are linked together that is interesting in the understanding of social pedagogic practice. This is illustrated in Figure 5.1. We can say that the relationship is the medium for the work with the client, the structure is where the work happens (though it also has characteristics of a medium) and change is the goal of the work. This trio of concepts represents a summary of the context where the social pedagogue works.

Figure 5.1: The social pedagogic context

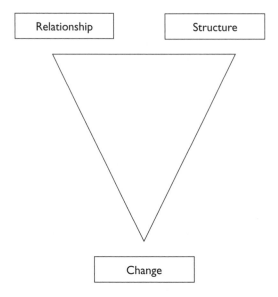

If we remove one of these elements, the social pedagogic context will also be gone. Social pedagogic work without a goal of change is paradoxical. If we remove the element of change, for example, in an institution, it would simply be a place where children and young people were kept. If the structure is omitted, we do not have an arena to work in. Then we would talk about being in a change-oriented relationship, which, in itself, might be useful. But it would not be social pedagogic, as the profession of social pedagogy is concerned with structure. Neither can we omit relationships. If we did, we would move into society's change-oriented work for larger groups, in other words, into the field of politics. Social pedagogic practice is inextricably linked to a personal dimension; the one who is being helped is the subject.

With this, I have established what I suggest we call the social pedagogic context. This is a practically oriented contextualisation, containing the necessary elements of the actual execution of the practice. This model describes a few fundamental elements in which all the elements need to be linked together, and not only that, but linked together in a particular way. The model could just as well be used in other professional fields, and, as such, it is in itself 'content non-specific'. It does not say anything about social pedagogy in particular. If we are to give it a social pedagogic content, this will have to be described, which is what I have tried to do in this chapter.

The concept of 'context' can be understood as something limited and almost physical. If we think about the context 'at home', we will, for example, often think about our own house. Durrant (1993) is also interested in context, and he describes it in a way that is interesting in a social constructionist perspective. His concept of context can be described as representing 'a framework for meanings that determines how people will make sense of a particular experience – what they think it is about' (Durrant, 1993, p 8). Here, it is meaning and not physical space that constitutes the understanding of context. I am suggesting, therefore, that the context where the social pedagogue works with clients (such as in an institution) is defined by all the assumptions that are produced by those present, which give meaning to the work they do together (cf Storø, 2005), and, thus, to their collaboration. The central aspect of this way of using the concept of 'context' is the element that creates meaning. Here, we find the link to social constructionism, and thereby also to social pedagogic practice as a language-based activity. It is through language-based actions (interaction) that we construct meaning. Using this way of thinking about the model in Figure 5.1, we can see that the relationships are awarded meaning by being played out in a structure, and by being perceived to be linked to the desire to work for change. This is how the concepts are linked together. What constitutes meaning in this construction, and therefore carries it on its back, is the combination of the elements relationship, structure and change.

Notes

[1] My apologies to dentists if I am guilty of oversimplifying their professional practice. I only know them as a patient. I would still stick my neck out and claim that social pedagogic work by nature is more complex and less predictable than the work of a dentist. I am, therefore, making the assumption that this is a valid comparison.

[2] Larsen's concept can be traced to psychological theory, even more precisely, to the psychodynamic tradition.

CHAPTER SIX

Where does the social pedagogue work?

We can find one answer to the question of where the social pedagogue works by looking at the various *workplaces* we can expect to come across him. I have previously mentioned that several groups of practitioners can be said to do social pedagogic work. This implies that there are many different workplaces where social pedagogic practice is carried out. I will start by looking at where we might find child welfare pedagogues.

The child welfare pedagogue's core workplaces have, for many years, been institutions, foster care services and municipal child welfare services. We can call these the first and second lines of child welfare. Child welfare pedagogues take care of tasks that are regulated by child welfare legislation. There has been a lot of discussion about whether to concentrate on first-line or second-line competencies in education and training. The former can be understood as competencies that are useful for working in the child welfare services (mainly in connection with casework based on the law), the latter as competencies that, first and foremost, are applicable in institutions (mainly milieu therapy). Both of these types of workplaces are important for child welfare pedagogues. It is also essential that an understanding of social pedagogy is deeply rooted in both places. Gradually, the recreation sector has also proved to be a central workplace for child welfare pedagogues. Youth clubs, outreach services and voluntary organisations that offer services to children and young people with special needs have become important places for child welfare pedagogues to work. Here, too, it is natural to envisage a social pedagogic foundation for the work.

The most recent arena for child welfare pedagogues is schools. Many schools have gradually understood the need for a coordinated preventive effort in everyday life in schools, and on particular efforts directed towards exposed individuals and groups among the pupils. *Environmental, or milieu therapist* is a new job description that, in some places, has been significant in terms of integration and the school's ability to identify pupils with special needs, in order to offer them something better that will increase their opportunities to benefit from the school's core activities. Child welfare pedagogues are also found in institutionalised day-care facilities for schoolchildren in Norway. We also come across this group of professionals in nursery schools. Social pedagogically oriented work in schools can be significant in terms of the inclusion of marginalised pupils and the prevention of such problems. We should also mention social educators. Their work with such people in their own homes often has clear social pedagogic characteristics.

We might also extend the understanding to various types of voluntary organisations, such as sports clubs, scouts and choirs. Such organisations mobilise a lot of people around their goal-oriented activities, but their work is often founded on what we could call social pedagogic ideas. In sport, and particularly team sports, inclusion in the community and collaboration around common goals are important attitude markers. However, there is an important distinction between social pedagogic practice and the practice we find, for example, in a sports team. If the trainer is working in a social pedagogic way, he will rarely know much about social pedagogic theory. *If* he does, it might be because he is coincidentally also a child welfare pedagogue. The social pedagogy-oriented theory applied by, for example, a football trainer will most probably be of a more general nature than the one applied by a trained social pedagogue. This does not mean that his work is less important, only that it is different.

We see that social pedagogic work can take place in many different places in society: in institutions for children and young people; in child welfare and social security offices; in schools; and in psychiatric units – as well as in the child's family and immediate environment.

Arenas

We get another answer to this chapter's question by looking at the arenas the social pedagogue moves in during his daily work. Erik Larsen suggests that work in a youth institution chiefly takes place in four arenas. These are shown in Figure 6.1.[1] The model mentions the youth institution as an arena, but it can also be used in other places where the social pedagogue works. Nevertheless, in the following, I have used the youth institution as a starting point in order to present a few practice examples.

What is striking when first looking at this model is that the pedagogic change-oriented work (some would call it *milieu* therapy) only constitutes a part of the total picture. The diversity of institutional everyday life also includes many other themes. In the context of an institution, we can say that the primary function of the work is *what the staff are doing*

Figure 6.1: Four arenas of social pedagogic work in a youth institution

WHAT ARE THE STAFF DOING WITH THE YOUNG PEOPLE? **THE PEDAGOGIC WORK TOWARDS CHANGE**	WHAT ARE THE STAFF DOING WITH THE STAFF? **THE COLLEGIAL DIALOGUE**
WHAT ARE THE YOUNG PEOPLE DOING WITH THE YOUNG PEOPLE? **THE NORMS AND INTERACTION AMONG THE YOUNG PEOPLE THEMSELVES**	WHAT ARE THE YOUNG PEOPLE DOING WITH THE STAFF? **THE INFLUENCE OF THE YOUNG PEOPLE**

with the young people. All the other tasks carried out by the staff are secondary functions. The collegial dialogue is an example. Other secondary tasks are meetings, budget planning, shift planning, report writing and so on. These are the sort of tasks that have to be carried out in order to enable work on the primary task. The young people's actions are described in the lower sections of the figure, and the staff's actions are described in the upper sections. The lower sections of the figure are, therefore, about what the young people are doing, and cannot be put into the categories of primary versus secondary tasks in the same way. Nevertheless, they are clearly *linked* to the primary professional task, as they belong to the social life of the institution. Work with how the young people influence each other and the staff, therefore, clearly belongs in the category of *pedagogic change-oriented work*, and, as such, must be regarded as a primary task.

Petter looks at his watch. The staff meeting has already been going on for an hour without getting to the matters he would like to discuss. They have been through an evaluation of the shift arrangements, they have talked about how the 24-hour reports could get better, and now they are in the middle of a discussion about expectations for the new supervisor. But when will they ever get to the point about next weekend's trip with the young people? And then the new, regular activity on Monday nights that he is going to be responsible for? These are the really important questions.

Milieu therapist Petter is activity-oriented. He appears to think that the most important thing you can do when working with vulnerable young people in an institution is to create opportunities for collaboration and to activate the young people. He has a good point; these are core situations in the work. But he risks losing an important perspective, which is about incorporating casual socialising and activities into a holistic understanding. If socialising with the young people is to have a value different from the socialising they have experienced previously, the staff need to have an understanding that goes beyond 'having a nice time'. Change-oriented work demands something more than that. When we look at the other components, it is easier to find the perspective that extends our understanding. On the other hand, it *may* be that Petter's colleagues are *too* preoccupied with the secondary tasks and, thereby, 'forget' what is primary. This is one of the dangers inherent in the organisation of social pedagogic work towards change: namely, regarding the actual organising as most important. Staff groups sometimes make the mistake of focusing more on what is required to deal with a task than on the task itself. Institutions may be well-run in the sense that all routines and structures are in good shape, but the work on creating a good social environment for change is not given sufficient priority. Managing workplaces where social pedagogic activity is practised requires a high degree of insight, not least in the balance between structure and content.

Leila is sitting at the other side of the table. She can see that Petter is impatient, and she knows that he wants to discuss his own items on the agenda. As a manager, she also knows that the discussion they are having about the new supervisor needs to be had today. The supervisor is coming next week, and it is important that they have agreed on the staff group's most important needs in terms of counselling. At the same time, Leila is concerned that the discussions about secondary topics should not be what the staff mostly have on their minds at the end of the meeting, in which case, they will not go back to the young people and make the best effort. She prepares to bring the discussion they are currently having to an end and proceed to the planning of the excursion and the Monday activities.

According to Larsen (2004), certain processes sometimes develop in a staff group where they do not seem to be concerned with the primary task. An example might be occasions where it appears more important to protect the staff against everyday problems than working with the children's and young people's processes of change. Pedagogic change-oriented work is a very complex process that demands a lot both from individual staff members, the whole staff group and management. Sometimes, staff in institutions develop their own needs, which have to be managed. These can be the needs: to understand what is happening; to have (as far as possible) a safe and predictable working day; to have an overall view; and to be able to trust one other. These are examples of staff needs that arise when working with people in crisis. Meeting these requirements is a very important professional task. However, they remain secondary in relation to the social pedagogue's primary tasks. In an institution, this needs to be emphasised, and frequently reiterated. Personally, it has given me great pleasure to work in institutions where it is frequently stated during professional discussions that 'in our institution, the young people come first'. This sentence is, in many ways, an operationalisation – in the form of a slogan – of the idea of the relationship between primary and secondary tasks.

In the model in Figure 6.1, the concrete work towards change is thematised through the question 'What are the staff doing with the young people?' An answer to this question would comprise all types of social pedagogic work with young people: activation, boundary-setting, the structuring of everyday life, conversations, meals, managed group processes, excursions and so on. I will come back to this in Chapter Seven, which deals with the social pedagogue's working tools. When we include what the staff are doing with *what the young people are doing* as a part of social pedagogic activity, we are talking about the more group-oriented part of milieu work. This is about the various types of more general gatherings arranged by the staff: the types of *in-between* situations that are characterised by clear interventions. This is what Petter appears to be most interested in. Is the dialogue between the adults and the young people open? Is it appreciative? Do the young people have opportunities to bring up suggestions or criticism? Are the adults and the young people doing lots of things together, or are they separated in everyday life at the institution? How do the adults and the young people communicate when they do things together? When are they not doing things together? Is there a good atmosphere? Does it feel safe to be a participant in this environment?

This book's perspective is that in a social pedagogic reality, one cannot *not* intervene. Everything the staff do must be understood as an intervention. It is not only the clear boundary-setting, the initiation of activities and organisation of everyday life that can be understood as interventions. The way adults talk to and treat young people can also be considered as interventions. It makes a difference whether the young person is treated with respect or not. This holistic view on the interaction between staff and young people tells us that being the adult is very demanding. Seen from the young people's point of view, it is quite natural that everything the adults do can be evaluated and criticised. They will quickly see through a practice where the adults are friendly and approachable in clear intervention situations, but not accessible during their coffee break, or a practice where one of the adults is interested in the young person's perspective in a group meeting, but not if they meet by chance outside the institution, when the adult is off work. For the young person, how exactly the adult behaves in the situations that are not the very core of the relationship between them is probably important.

Both fields in the lower sections of Figure 6.1 are about what the young people do. We know that when children and young people come together in an institution, social situations and collaboration will occur between them. In a study in a children's home, Fransson (1996) found that the girls at the institution related to a girl community that had its own culture.[2] This is also known from other types of institutions, such as hospitals (Album, 1996). Fransson writes about the community of young girls as one of several cultures at the institution. But this community also consisted of several smaller groups, which, according to Fransson (1996, p 41), functioned as a 'unit which separates itself from the milieu therapists'. At the same time, this study shows that the community does not exist as a predictable unit all the time. The contact between the girls varies from day to day, and Fransson writes that it is difficult to talk about a 'group' in the strict sense. We begin to see that living in an institution can be regarded as a constant process of negotiation about which resident culture is to be predominant. Sometimes, it is positive and supportive; other times, difficult to be a part of. It also varies within the context of *us and the staff*. Some days, it is characterised by cooperation and ease; other days, the young people can form more or less conscious counter-cultures, implying a protest against the adults/social pedagogues (Garsjø, 2003).

What the young people are doing together is both natural friendship, joint participation in activities and group formation around common interests. At the same time, it is often easy to spot negative interaction: the development of negative norms; interaction linked to common negative experiences; and the formation of negative subcultures that do not follow the norms of either the institution or society as a whole. Andreassen (2003) emphasises this in his review of research at institutions for young people with behavioural problems. In the field of *social pedagogic change-oriented work*, we must, therefore, also include *what the staff do with what the young people do*. The staff at an institution must have a particular interest in what goes on between those who live there. All aspects of the institution, including this one, are learning arenas for the young people. They learn from each other, not least in parallel interaction with the adults. This implies that the adults have the opportunity to observe how the young people collaborate with each other, and then intervene on the basis of what they see.

> At the young people's home, the staff had been observing that the residents were irritable and not very accessible to the adults in certain situations for some weeks. Through discussions in the staff group, conversations with the young people and observation of daily life at the institution, they had reached the conclusion that they had to intervene on several fronts. Leila had asked everybody to be particularly alert as to whether a drug culture was about to develop after the new girl had moved in. At the same time, she had been positive towards Petter's suggestion of arranging an excursion to the mountains and to improve the range of activities on Mondays.

In situations where the community of young people becomes a more important focus than individual change-oriented work, the staff of an institution often find themselves in a state of readiness. I will return to this in Chapter Seven.

The model in Figure 6.1 concentrates on the internal life of an institution. Much of the criticism directed at institutions is about their tendency to be closed to the outside world. If an institution shuts itself off, there is a danger that the rest of the community will be sceptical about it, and this scepticism can rub off on the residents (Garsjø, 2003). In addition, the residents will not get much stimulus from 'normal life' and the social learning situations it offers, situations they almost invariably have to return to sooner or later. In order to counteract this type of problem, it is important to open up the institution to the outside world. Society can get an insight into institutions through supervision and inspection arrangements, but it is also important that everybody who comes into contact with an institution in its daily life has the opportunity to learn about what is happening there. A fifth arena ought, therefore, to be added: namely, work done by the staff with parents, networks, the local environment and cooperation partners. This is illustrated at the top of Figure 6.2.

In addition, we can find a sixth arena by focusing on giving those who live there opportunities for interaction with others, both while they are there and after they have moved out. The fifth and sixth arenas point outwards into society for those living in institutions. Their stay will come to an end at some point, and it is necessary, therefore, for the clients to have active contact with the outside world along the way. The sixth arena for the social pedagogue's practice is included at the bottom of Figure 6.2.

In other words, the social pedagogue's arenas can be identified on the basis of his workplace, but also on the practice arenas he moves in during his daily work, as we have seen in this chapter.

Figure 6.2: Six arenas for social pedagogic work in an institution

WHAT ARE THE STAFF DOING WITH THE OUTSIDE WORLD? **WORK WITH FAMILIES, NETWORKS, THE LOCAL ENVIRONMENT AND COOPERATION PARTNERS**	
WHAT ARE THE STAFF DOING WITH THE YOUNG PEOPLE? **THE PEDAGOGIC WORK TOWARDS CHANGE**	WHAT ARE THE STAFF DOING WITH THE STAFF? **THE COLLEGIAL DIALOGUE**
WHAT ARE THE YOUNG PEOPLE DOING WITH THE YOUNG PEOPLE? **THE NORMS AND INTERACTION AMONG THE YOUNG PEOPLE THEMSELVES**	WHAT ARE THE YOUNG PEOPLE DOING WITH THE STAFF? **THE INFLUENCE OF THE YOUNG PEOPLE**
WHAT ARE THE YOUNG PEOPLE DOING WITH THE OUTSIDE WORLD? **THE YOUNG PEOPLE'S INTERACTION WITH SOCIAL NETWORKS AND THE LOCAL ENVIRONMENT**	

Notes

[1] As far as I know, this model has not been previously published, but only presented in lecture format. My model is a reworking of Larsen's original model. His concepts were developed in a psychologically oriented treatment tradition. I have replaced some of these with pedagogically oriented concepts.

[2] There were only girls living at this institution, and the study therefore chose girls.

CHAPTER SEVEN

What are the tools of the social pedagogue's trade?

I have previously mentioned that, in my view, there is no homogeneous set of social pedagogic methods. It is not possible to write one complete manual comprising all the different methodical challenges facing the social pedagogue in his everyday practice. Social pedagogic practice is diverse, complex and contextual. Nevertheless, my aim with this chapter is to describe social pedagogic methods. It is my intention to provide examples of methods and strategies that I perceive as social pedagogic. It is up to the reader to find a way to apply them in the practical reality in which he or she finds themself. I hope that they will be useful sources of inspiration for local method development wherever the individual social pedagogue may be. I have chosen to give general methodical descriptions at the beginning of the chapter, and then to describe some locally based methods towards the end.

Systematic activity

In the introduction to my description of the methodical element of social pedagogic practice, I would like to stress that this practice must be regarded as a systematic activity. This is something I have barely touched on earlier in the book. It is probably fairly clear from many of the descriptions in the various chapters, but I will mention the point again here. I have talked about the necessity of practice being *informed*, which implies that it is governed by both theory and values. I have also written about relationships and humanity. Closeness and involvement with the clients combined with a considered and reflected professionalism could be considered close to the ideal. A systematic and planned effort contributes to giving social pedagogic assistance its professional status. This is where we see that social pedagogic practice has a scientific element and is not just linked to what I call ordinary interaction. There is nearly always an element of planning, implementation and evaluation, which are signs of considered professional activities, as opposed to an arbitrary series of interventions. Several authors suggest working in accordance with a systematic model (Kvaran, 1996; Grønvold, 1997; Linde and Nordlund, 2006). There are a number of such models, but most of them involve thinking of the work in phases. Normally, the first phase would be problem definition, mapping and goal formulation. Phases of planning interventions and then implementing them would follow. The last phase normally has an evaluation function, often where both the result of the interventions and the actual work process are subjected to assessment. This type of model is often presented as circular, where the phases are illustrated by the drawing of a circle. The last phase, the evaluation phase, is thus not only the 'last phase', but also the 'first phase' in the next round of the systematic work process. This is a clear illustration of the fact that social pedagogic work should be seen as part of a continuous process of learning and improvement taking us ever nearer to our professional goals.

Producing professional documentation

A systematic work effort usually involves 'getting something down on paper'. The social pedagogue has to expect that some of his work will involve writing. He writes reports, letters, minutes of meetings and sometimes other documents. For most newly trained social pedagogues, report-writing is their first encounter with producing professional documentation. Many are unsure how to do this, and help and training from colleagues are not always easily available. Many social pedagogue practitioners are worried about writing; they feel more secure with handling the purely practical part of their profession than the aspect that concerns putting things down on paper. My own experience is that you learn a lot in your profession when writing, be it reports or other specialist documents. However, for many, writing is a barrier that needs to be broken down in order to get started.

Language

Social pedagogic work towards change is, to a large extent, a language-based activity (Berglund, 2004). Language is the medium whereby we communicate and receive communication from our clients, and from each other as professionals. According to Lundby (1998, p 75), social constructionist theorists look 'at ideas, perceptions and memories as emerging from social interaction and negotiated through language'. We can say, therefore, that language is a tool of the trade. Language has many functions, and I will look at concepts, communication and conversations in particular. Language is reckoned to be the most important arena for social interaction for the social constructionist-oriented professional. Burr (2003) perceives language as a form of action. In this socially oriented perspective, it is natural to talk about interaction, which gives us the concept that acting together – linguistically and in other ways – provides the opportunity for change and development. The acknowledgement that language can be seen as an 'interactive process' (Lundby, 1998, p 81) points in the direction of the social pedagogue's core activity. In the linguistic interaction that takes place between the social pedagogue and his client(s), language is rarely or never used in an arbitrary way – at least not if the social pedagogue is a true professional. There will always be some ethical ground rules for professional language. It should be unambiguous, non-judgemental and accessible. I will not elaborate too much on these aspects of language as they are dealt with in technical publications on communication and ethics. In this context, I am more interested in how to work on language in order for it to function pedagogically. The social pedagogy-oriented author Stig-Arne Berglund (2004, p 142) thinks that the linguistic activities of the social pedagogue are central when he writes that 'the self [is] continually being constructed, assessed and reconstructed in the social language interplay of everyday situations'. Anne Jansen (2007, p 46), who is interested in how we present ourselves through narratives, writes the following from a social constructionist psychological viewpoint:

> How do we create ourselves through the stories we tell? We use events in our lives, what we have done, the experiences we have had, we put them together and interpret them. However, creating oneself through stories is not a lonely or private affair. The stories do not stand alone – they also need to relate to previously told stories and the stories of others, and as such they are part of a network. We tell stories to others and receive additions and corrections both to what we claim as fact and to our interpretations of it. Sometimes stories are confirmed, other times they are rejected.

It is particularly when we get to the question of language that we can see the social constructionist way of thinking translated into practical action. As previously mentioned, a modernist way of thinking involves seeing reality as an objective entity ready and waiting to be discovered. On the other hand, a postmodern and, thereby, also, social constructionist perspective implies understanding reality as something we create through the use of language. In our 'internal conversations' with ourselves and our social conversations with each other, we develop our knowledge, our view of ourselves and each other, and our problem-solving strategies. In other words, reality is not understood as something objective that exists outside humans, but something that we construct in social processes. The most important aspect of these processes is that they are language-based. Howe (1993) stresses that the opportunity to engage in an active conversation about oneself creates a basis for self-understanding, and, thereby, for change. In particular, he sees language as a key to creating meaning, and to having control over the process of creating meaning.

Social pedagogic practice is diverse. Sometimes, it is hard to understand. What are core situations to an adult may appear less important to a child or young person. Maybe young people are more interested in being treated well than in discussing a new boundary-setting situation. In this way, what may seem to be core situations for one person might, for another, be situations on the edge of what is natural or desirable to be interested in. We can talk here about a possible disparity in the perception of what is a core question and what is peripheral. It is not difficult to imagine that different perceptions of what is important make the work of helping people difficult. Through language, we can find our way to the perceptions of different actors. But are perceptions really something we *have*? In a constructionist perspective, it would be insufficient to think in this way about people's assumptions, perceptions or opinions. Rather, perceptions should be regarded as constructions that one *makes*. The phenomenon 'perceptions' is not about owning perceptions, but about *forming* them. This way of thinking is dynamic, as we are also saying that perceptions change. The social constructionist would say that such dynamic processes of change take place in the social space that we jointly construct when we act together. Such co-constructions must necessarily, to a large extent, happen through language, as so much of our interaction and collaboration is done through language. With this, I have linked the concepts of language and action; what I am saying is that we can think of language as linguistic actions.

When we look at the social pedagogue's linguistic actions, we can focus on which of these actions promote the professional effort, and which of them hinder it. If linguistic actions are to be dynamic, they must be designed to promote dialogue. The dynamism is achieved by both communicating parties being given the opportunity to participate and influence. In a dialogue between the social pedagogue and the client, it is thus essential that the client is given a chance to speak. But it is not enough that he is heard. He must also be taken seriously. If linguistic interaction is to provide openings and not close things down, the social pedagogue must make it clear that there are different ways to perceive the situation, and that the client's construction has equal value to that of the social pedagogue.

We can describe a meeting of two people as a meeting of two different perspectives: the first person's perspective and the second person's perspective. In such a situation, the ideal would be to adopt a decentred perspective. This implies including the perspectives of several of the interacting parties; in this case, both the child/young person and the adult. It is the responsibility of the adult to demonstrate this way of thinking. Then the young person must be helped to understand that what the adult is doing is also important. Røkenes and Hansen (2006) write that good conversations must be both anchored in a common world and strive to widen perspectives. It is the latter function that makes the conversation dynamic and provides opportunities to explore new ways of thinking, to find new constructions.

The bilingual social pedagogue

In all conversations, from everyday to technical ones, we use concepts to explain what we want to express. It is often useful to distinguish 'term' from 'concept': 'term' is the actual word, while 'concept' is the expression of the content we give to the word. It is not very hard to agree on a term, perhaps with the exception of how to pronounce it. But there may well be greater uncertainty and disagreement about the concepts connected with the term. Some terms have several conceptual meanings, and which one we use is not arbitrary. We can perceive concepts as words with a lot of content, and that the content is value-laden. This value-loading is interesting. Some words are not particularly value-laden; they usually describe concrete things, such as 'chair' or 'air'. We may, of course, have different concepts for the term 'air' depending on what we are talking about, but, most of the time, clarification is unnecessary. Let us have a look at the term 'social pedagogy'. For some, the conceptual meaning of this term has to do with a perspective for understanding mechanisms in society for inclusion and exclusion (cf Madsen, 2006). For others (myself included), the term describes to a greater extent methods in the work with children and young people (though in such a way that this work is *linked* to the former interpretation). We witnessed these differences in conceptual meaning in the conversation between Trond and Mette in the first chapter of this book. The question of which sense of the word one relates to is also value-laden. Mette was interested in the wider context, while Trond was preoccupied with concrete matters relating to individuals.

In his daily practice, the social pedagogue uses concepts that arise from theories that are both full of content and value-laden, and also an everyday-oriented language without these special components. This duality constitutes one particular aspect of the social pedagogue's professional competence. It makes our movement between the different arenas visible, for example, when we go from a conference room to the playroom in an institution. When we work with children and young people, we normally use everyday language to speak *to* them, while we talk *about* them in a language filled with specialist terminology.

Pål has spent the evening with the young person, Wahid, for whom he is the environmental contact person at the residential home. They have had a nice evening together, and Pål tells Wahid that he feels that he has got to know him well during the weeks that he has been living at the home. Towards the end of the evening, he is sitting with a colleague, summing up what happened during the day. Pål says that he feels that the building of a relationship with Wahid functions pretty well, and this leads to a discussion about whether the boy is making use of the offer of adult contact.

Specialist language is often more concise than the language we use to talk to our clients. Specialist words are often clearly defined and with a specific meaning. This implies that we can talk about the clients and the work we are doing with them with less danger of being misunderstood than if we were only using everyday language. Specialist language fine-tunes the linguistic deliverances between collaborating colleagues. We can say, therefore, that it is ethically most responsible to learn the required specialist terms and concepts and to use them in situations where they belong.

Another aspect of the social pedagogue's bilingualism is, thus, that he must live up to the demands of adjusting to the client and his linguistic world. This implies that the social pedagogue must put the specialist terms to one side and start using everyday language when he is talking to the client. In *some* situations, this is relatively easy, for example, when they are talking about everyday matters. In other situations, it can be much more difficult; namely, when the social pedagogue has to talk to the client regarding topics about which he also has a professional dialogue with his colleagues. It may be that the content of a professional discussion needs to be communicated to the client in such a way that he understands what *he* needs to understand.

> One day Pål says to Wahid that he would like to talk to him. They sit down after supper, and Pål says to Wahid that he wants to tell him what he has been discussing with the other milieu therapists at the institution. The previous day, at the staff meeting, a discussion arose about what several perceived as Wahid's reluctance to develop close contact with others. It was decided to observe everyday situations where this situation might arise during the following week. In his conversation with Wahid, Pål says that he would like them to do some activities together, and that he really would like to get to know Wahid better. He tells him that he thinks Wahid needs to spend time with other people and do things with others.

Some social pedagogues argue for the advantage of not being 'bilingual'. In other words, they would like the same concepts and speech used in conversations with the client to be predominant in dialogue with colleagues. It is often argued that social pedagogues who use specialist language risk distancing themselves from the client and his world of experiences. In the long term, it is difficult to defend this standpoint. The ideal of 'being where the client is' is a good and important professional ideal. Nevertheless, it is difficult to stick solely to the 'near-the-client' position if we are to fulfil our role as professionals. The social pedagogue's professionalism demands that he also adopts a role that is characterised by distance. This is necessary in order to have the opportunity to analyse and give something back to the client in a way that is not only based on emotion. It is consideration for the client that tips the balance towards such an acknowledgement. The social pedagogue must not only be 'bilingual', he must also be 'bi-contextual'. With that, I mean that he must be able to understand the client's context, and he must be able to leave that and place himself in the professional's context. The former implies empathy with the client's situation; the latter contributes to positive change by regarding the client from *another* standpoint. The client has a right to be presented with a viewpoint other than his own.

It is easy to see that nearness to the client is an ideal. But the client also has a right to help from a person who understands the importance of regarding the problem with 'fresh eyes'. When the client asks for help from the professional, the professional would let the client down if he were unable to offer more than just 'I *really* understand what you mean'. For the professional to be able to do this, he needs to move into a different context, into his own professional context. From there, he can analyse and work out strategies that can be presented to the client in the next round. Those who claim that specialist language creates a distance to the client's world of experiences are right. That is precisely one of its purposes: creating the necessary distance. It does not mean that the social pedagogue should show less empathy or be less interested in listening to the client. On the contrary, the distance *enables* the social pedagogue to offer nearness as well. It would be naive to think that a social pedagogue can offer nearness and empathy to many clients during a long professional career if he does not, at the same time, look after his own need for reflection. This is where specialist language comes in as something that helps the social pedagogue to preserve himself and his own integrity.

Specialist language is carefully weighed, substantial and content-rich. Specialist terms are not something that a professional dreams up at a moment's notice; rather, they have developed over time in dialogue between many professional practitioners. They are founded on research and through being criticised in specialist debates. 'Formation' is one such term. It has a long history, and must be regarded as a rock-solid term in the profession. Among professionals, it is a working tool that helps them arrive at an understanding that will benefit the client. However, the social pedagogue rarely uses the term in direct conversation with the client. He would not say: 'You need to go through processes of formation.' Rather, he would say something like: 'It is important that you spend time with friends in order to play a part in the community and learn what people in your new environment do and what they like. In that way, you may find it easier to make new friends.' The specialist language is an expression of theory and methods, but also of knowledge in the professional field that has been developed to help clients. The social pedagogue who does not use specialist language risks letting his client down. A working tool in the form of this specialist language is available to him, and he has a practical and moral obligation to use it.

Let us briefly have a look at the ideal of being close to the client's linguistic world. As previously mentioned, this ideal is a good one. The person who is helping someone else needs to approach the other person's world of experiences, and experiences are captured in our language. The communication process with the other person, in our case, the client, is essential in order to be able to carry out a good professional job. We need to do more than just plan for good interventions. We must also be able to talk to the client about the intervention, and explain the thought processes that lead to it. This communication must happen in such a way that the client understands what we mean. It is not sufficient to explain to the client what the specialist terms actually mean. We need to explain using the kind of language that the client understands straight away. Anything else would cause the client to feel alienated from his own situation.

It is difficult to give this important field complete justice in this book. I would have had to use more space than I have at my disposal. Therefore, I have chosen to mention the topic of communication as one of the most important tools for social pedagogic work. I have also chosen to refer to the literature that deals with this in a sufficiently thorough way.

Conversations

Obviously, setting up a conversation is one possible form of action. As, to a large extent, the social pedagogue utilises language, a conversation is the most important medium for linguistic action. A conversation can be broadly defined as any occasion that involves linguistic interaction between people. However, in this chapter, I will limit the concept of conversation to mean the situations where the social pedagogue arranges to sit down and talk to the client about something in particular. Such a conversation can take place in the common room of an institution, by a bedside, in the car, in the kitchen, at the youth club, during a walk and so on. The conversation may, of course, also have been initiated by the client; in which case, at first, it will not be a social pedagogic action, but might well develop in such a way that it assumes the characteristics of such an action.

Conversations can be more or less structured, more or less goal-oriented, and more or less focused. In everyday life at an institution, you will be able to spot many different kinds of conversations.

Abdi has decided to have a chat with Tommy, for whom he is the contact person. Tommy has lived at the residential home for a few months, and Abdi feels that it is about time they talk about the fact that Tommy does not do anything outside the home. Abdi tells Tommy that he would like to talk to him after supper. They find a quiet corner in order not to be disturbed. However, it becomes apparent that Tommy is not very communicative this evening. Abdi has to force the words out of him, and, after a while, he decides to postpone the whole thing. A few days later, he is given a fresh opportunity while they are driving back to the home after a visit to the cinema.

Abdi's decision to have this conversation later in a far less structured and focused context is probably a result of his experience as a social pedagogue and milieu therapist over many years. For Abdi, milieu work is not about 'winning' a situation, but, rather, about managing to have the dialogue he feels is necessary over a period of time. This is probably a good idea. One of the reasons could be that the actual structure can be an obstacle to the breakthrough of the pedagogical element. Maybe Tommy was not especially willing to say anything that evening because he felt pressured to say something in particular? Another reason could be that everyday life in an institution includes a lot of situations that can give rise to conversations, and Abdi counted on being able to talk to Tommy in the next few days anyway. Maybe what happened was simply for the best. Maybe the aborted conversation was necessary in order to introduce the topic to Tommy, and leave it to him to decide when he was ready to have this chat. It is possible for Abdi to think in this way because the institutional context gives him several potential situations where the work can be continued.

One of Abdi's responsibilities is to arrange the weekly meeting with the young residents at the institution. In the light of his work with Tommy and possible activities for him, Abdi decides to use the next meeting to talk to all the young people about activities.

Conversations can also be arranged with groups of clients. Such conversations can be structured, or more open. In an institutional context, they are often characterised by being attitude-oriented, and they therefore contribute to the development of norms and expectations in a constant process.

Pedagogic conversations about fairness

What is pedagogic in the social pedagogue's way of talking? That is what I shall discuss in this chapter.

Children and young people are often very preoccupied with what is fair or not. That is, of course, also the case with the children and young people with whom social pedagogues work, perhaps particularly so in their case. These children come from different family situations, but, up to a point, they have to be treated in the same way in the contexts where they meet with the social pedagogue. Children and young people who come into contact with social pedagogues are often very aware of how they are treated by these adults. This is particularly true for the children and young people who move into institutions. Discussions about fairness are especially relevant for distinguishing between what is pedagogic and what is not. We are therefore going to take a closer look at these conversations.

When the social pedagogue is challenged by children and young people who are calling for fairness, this is often an issue of equal treatment. A common question may be: 'Why I am not allowed when he was?' In such situations, it is easy to be put under pressure and try to work things out in such a way that everyone gets the same treatment. This is often a poor strategy. You should, of course, listen to children who feel that they have been badly treated in one way or another. However, the answer to such questions is often something other than trying to treat the children the same. We can reserve equal treatment for straightforward and clear situations, such as how much pocket money the children in an institution should have, or that the foster child and the foster family's own children should have an equal share of domestic duties.

Other, more complex questions, like how often children in a residential home should be allowed to go home to their parents at the weekend, cannot be decided on the basis of equal treatment. What matters here are individual needs, and they often have to be seen in relation to many other factors. If we are talking about home weekends, the parental situation, what has happened during previous visits and so on are normally central questions in the assessment.[1]

This implies that in many situations, equal treatment and fair treatment will be incompatible. It is important to emphasise this at a time when our eyes have been opened to the importance of user contribution. The reasoning is that different individuals have different needs. In other words, user contribution in social pedagogic work with children and young people must not be reduced to a question of equal treatment. We are therefore required to assess the needs and situation of each individual in a wider context before making decisions regarding questions where there is a demand for equal treatment. Personally, I have often found the following phrase useful, which I have uttered to both children and young people I have worked with, but also to myself when I have faced a difficult decision: 'Treating people equally is really unfair'. I have then followed this up with an explanation based on the same logic as I have used in this section of the book.

In the work of the social pedagogue practitioner, such conversations with children and young people constitute very central components of the daily interaction with clients. The most important element in this type of conversation is not necessarily always the decision or outcome of the discussion. It is often the actual conversation about several possible decisions or outcomes that determines whether we can talk about a good social pedagogic situation. The social pedagogue has a pedagogic slant on his work, which includes teaching children and young people to make decisions themselves, weighing up various pros and cons, addressing dilemmas with reflection, and so on. At the same time, we should sound a warning against misuse of situations where a decision is needed. The process-oriented social pedagogue may be in danger of being too preoccupied with processes and the possibilities, limitations and (not least) consequences offered by various choices. Most of us have met someone who constantly reflects on various alternatives and never reaches a decision, and we know how irritating it is to be dependent on decisions that are supposed to be made by this person. Treating clients in this way is perhaps a particularly strong tradition within psychology-oriented professional practice. We all know the joke about the patient who asks the psychologist about something for which a clear answer is definitely required, and gets the woolly reply: 'Well ... what do *you* think?' Based on this reasoning, we can say that there is a time for reflection and negotiation, but also a time for making decisions about the questions that are being discussed.

Practical interventions

Social pedagogic work is language-based, but is not *only* about linguistic actions. There are many ways to carry out this practice, many other types of intervention. One obvious possibility for the social pedagogue is to facilitate and direct various situations and events that he feels may have a developmental and changing effect on children and young people. In this section, I shall look at some of the various alternatives for action available to the social pedagogue. The alternatives are numerous, so the purpose of this list is to give some examples of what a social pedagogic intervention *might* be.

Working with groups

In much of this book, I write about 'the client' in the singular. But social pedagogues also meet with clients in groups. It might be the children's group at the school day-care facility, the youth group at an institution or all the young people one comes into contact with in outreach activities. Of these three, the first two are more defined, and the last less defined. When the social pedagogue meets groups of children, he must alternate all the time between relating to each child individually and relating to the whole group. Work with individuals in a group normally arises from each individual's needs. When a group becomes the object of a social pedagogue's interest, the focus changes. If the social pedagogue chooses to work with a group, norms and regulations for group life are often the theme. This may be expressed or not expressed by the social pedagogue. The social pedagogic effort often seeks to create conditions for the inclusion of all group members. In such cases, it may be necessary to throw some light on the members' attitudes to each other. One example of this would be a teacher's work on the class environment.

One important point is that you can work with a group either directly or via individual members. When a group is new, it is often necessary to work with it collectively. The purpose in such cases is usually to contribute to 'defining' the group. By that, I mean making it clear to the participants that they are actually part of a group, and that they should be aware of the agreements, norms and regulations that hold it together.

It is often useful for children and young people with differing social problems to gain new experiences in terms of relationship, structure and changes within a group. Only then can the social pedagogue start talking about the experiences made by individual members and the group as a whole – and this is subsequently transformed into educational material. Children and young people can also learn to support each other through participation in such groups.

Activities

Another kind of group-oriented work can be seen when the social pedagogue is running activities for a group of children or young people, or planning for a group to doing something nice together, achieve something or carry out a piece of work together. The aim of group work with these goals is usually to give the participants an idea of what several people can achieve if they all pull together, or that they can have a nice time when they interact in a good way. At the same time, it is both possible and right to focus on individual activities.

There are several reasons why activities can be described as an important arena in social pedagogic work. To sum up briefly, we can say that one of the main reasons is that this is an arena where children and young people actually find themselves. If he looks for them, this is where the social pedagogue will find them. In other words, this arena belongs to the children and young people, and it is natural for it to be incorporated into the social pedagogue's field of interest. The other main reason is that activities represent an arena where much of the social pedagogue's core activity can be useful. Activities are, for example, an arena for learning and mastering, including the learning and mastering of skills (Nybø, 1999).

When children and young people carry out activities, it is often the actual activity itself that is seen as valuable. Nybø (1999) writes that the social pedagogue's aim with the activity is, first and foremost, to initiate the clients' own activity.

One important aspect of the relationship of activities to learning is that the actual activity often has norms and rules that the children and young people have to learn in order to be able to carry it out. This learning goes beyond the activity itself; through the activity, you learn things that will come in useful in other places and other contexts. It is easiest to spot this when looking at group activities, such as playing football or hopscotch. Norms and rules in the actual activities teach the children to cooperate, await their turn, make an effort to reach a goal and so on. These are skills that the child needs in many situations other than the actual game. By learning skills about how to carry out the activities, children and young people will also learn about social life in general. So, activities are something you can do in order to have a good time, and to practise social competence. We could call this collaboration competence. Learning to collaborate with other people is important in order to increase the opportunities for inclusion in a community. Social competence can be understood as something that goes beyond the skills level. Rather, this type of competence should be regarded as a holistic framework that includes social awareness and how to use it in collaboration with others (cf Ogden, 1995). Gresham and Elliott (1984, recounted in Ogden, 1997) give five main areas of social competence:

- Cooperation – sharing with others, helping others, following rules, dealing with messages.
- Self-assertion – asking others for information, presenting one's point of view, reacting to other people's actions.
- Self-control – ability to wait one's turn, ability to compromise, reacting appropriately to being teased.
- Empathy – showing consideration and respect for other people's feelings and opinions.
- Responsibility – communicating with adults, showing respect for property and work.

We can see the importance attached to the social side of all these areas of competence. Through participation in activities, the child/young person is given good opportunities to practise all these elements. Those who are socially competent acquire access to the community by mastering what is needed for inclusion.

We can define the concept of activity fairly broadly by saying that everything people do constitutes activity. In a way, this would fit in with social pedagogic thinking, which is broad and comprehensive. But wide concepts are also problematic because they describe 'everything' and, therefore, tell us little. We could, for example, include schoolwork and even sleeping in the concept 'activity' if we define it this broadly. That would be reasonable if we simply say that activities are things people *do*. But I want to set limits to this. When I write about activities in this book, I mean play, hobbies, games and other leisure-oriented transactions. Some such activities can, of course, take place in contexts other than leisure, such as at school, but that is a less important point. It is probably reasonable to include more duty-oriented activities in this concept, such as cooking, tidying one's room, mowing the lawn and so on. Activities understood as leisure go on constantly in the lives of children and young people. They constitute one of the most important arenas where children and young people find themselves. Through activities, they meet others, but they also encounter themselves. By this, I mean that they find out things about themselves through *doing*. Of course, activities also provide the opportunity to have fun and relax. The recreational aspect of the activity is no less important than the educational. Social pedagogic work is often fairly serious. In order for the social pedagogue to even manage to get contact with the people he has to work with, he must include playing and activities in his professional practice. At the same time, we should remember that play has its own inherent value:

> We should ask ourselves: are we playing enough with the young people we work with? There are plenty of deadly serious young people with difficult lives who have forgotten how to play. And there are plenty of deadly serious social workers who have also forgotten how to play. We cannot only have conversations and meetings. We also need to play. We will then teach the young people this really important thing which is recreation. I am not thinking of recreation as passivity – not doing anything. I am thinking of recreation as something you do simply for the sake of pleasure, in such a way that you have a natural break in the work with your life problems. (Storø, 1997)

Departments that train child welfare pedagogues understand this. They include the unique subject 'activity studies', which is hardly found in any other university or college department. When visiting some of these child welfare courses, you can come across adults learning to play the guitar, using climbing walls, doing photography or collating pictures using different materials. They learn not only to carry out these various activities, but also how to work with children and young people via these activities.

I suggested earlier that the social pedagogue might go to the activity arena and find the children or young people there. This can be understood on two levels. One is concrete: the social pedagogue must be willing to meet children where they actually are, such as in a playground, on a football pitch or in front of a computer. When we adults decide to work with children, we must be willing to consider physically relocating ourselves from the office to the playground. Adult activity of the professional kind also has its arenas. In addition to the office, we find adult activities in the staffroom, the conference room, the therapy room or the classroom. But as children and young people have their own activities, it is natural for the social pedagogue to move some of *his* activity to where they are. The second level of *finding* children or young people is finding them in a more figurative sense – about going with them into their world. The social pedagogue needs both the conviction that this is important and the ability to carry it out. The way I see it is that the analytically oriented adult cannot fill the role of social pedagogue alone. He needs to be accompanied by the playful adult.

Seen from the social pedagogue's point of view, it might be interesting to distinguish between two different types of learning in connection with activities: facilitated and directed learning; and 'random' or integral learning. Let us look at them in turn. Activities can be arranged with the aim of teaching children and young people certain skills or other things.

> Kirsti is a milieu therapist in a school. One of her tasks is to arrange a gathering of a few selected young girls every Monday. One of the activities Kirsti is planning is for all the participants to be seated around the table at the start of the group meeting. Then they will each talk a little bit about what they have been doing over the weekend. Kirsti's thinking behind this part of the group activity is that the girls, who are all fairly withdrawn, should practise introducing themselves and talking about themselves to other people.

A lot of learning through activities is 'random', that is, not directed by an adult. I am using inverted commas here in order to hint that this learning is not really arbitrary. At least it is not arbitrary in the sense that it happens completely haphazardly, though we can say that it is arbitrary in the sense that it is not planned. This type of learning can also occur during activities, and it often does, but not always. It is built into the activity, but not in a planned and (adult-)directed way. Free play is one such activity. When children are playing freely in a sandpit, they learn how to collaborate, for example, by building a sandcastle. But the children may also sit by themselves and play in their own little corners of the sandpit. If that is the case, this learning opportunity will be lost; at least on that occasion. In itself, this is completely unproblematic. Play has many functions, and learning is only one of them. Other functions can be having a nice time, relaxing and just being with others. It is important to bear this in mind. Social pedagogues occasionally become a little too eager on pedagogy's behalf. They strive to provide for learning 'the whole time', and may not see the importance of free play.

> Kirsti is having a discussion with her colleague Harald, who works at the school's day-care facility. Harald would like to start an activity to teach some of the most active and restless boys to show consideration towards each other. He knows about Kirsti's girl gathering, and feels that it would be useful to do something similar for four of the 10-year-old boys. One of the form teachers has been talking about a problem with bullying. Kirsti says that she thinks Harald ought to find something other than a conversation-based group for these boys. She feels that they would not benefit from a managed group like that, and especially not at the end of a long school day. She suggests, instead, that Harald should take the boys with him into the woods and build a tree house with them. She recommends that Harald arrange an activity where

cooperation and the fun of creating something are most important. She says that she thinks the boys would benefit more from this.

Another point in Kirsti's suggestion is that activities create collaboration between those who participate. Positive collaboration situations are valuable for all children and young people (and also, for that matter, for adults). In particular, children and young people with some kind of problem in their lives will benefit from experiencing positive collaboration with other children and with adults (Larsen, 2004). In such positive situations with adults who are also social pedagogues, children from difficult backgrounds can experience a feeling of being cared for and included. At its best, they can experience that their mastering is seen and confirmed, and they can see that the adults take pleasure in both the actual activity and being together during the activity. Adults who are involved in an activity that they enjoy themselves while interacting with children can often give out a great deal of positive energy and inspiration.

One of the fundamental understandings of social pedagogy is the importance of working towards the inclusion of people in society and countering marginalisation and exclusion. Play and other activities often include situations where these concepts can be used. Playing children know something about inclusion and exclusion. They also know something about being included and excluded. This means that play is important for the development of attitudes about caring for other people. Organised group activities with rules, such as ball games, include many situations that give children and young people 'free' training in these functions. Sometimes, the social pedagogue needs to step in when children and young people experience being pushed out of the group.

Ever since she started working as a milieu therapist in the school, Kirsti has focused on situations where one or several of the pupils might feel excluded. One day, she finds Tine alone at the end of a corridor. As the school day had ended half an hour earlier, Kirsti feels that there must be a reason why Tine is still at school and that she, as a milieu therapist, ought to find out what it is. She goes up to Tine to talk to her.

Some activities and activity arenas are changing. Such changes are felt by the people doing the activities, but not necessarily by others. The Internet and other uses of information and communication technologies (ICT) are examples of such arenas. Children and young people often know about the new ways to use these arenas, while adults have to actively work to get to know them and understand how they are changing. It is important for adults to have knowledge of children's activities and leisure arenas. One of the reasons for this is that they can use the knowledge to regulate the arena and the activity itself. Another reason is that it is necessary to know the arenas children and young people move in to be able to communicate well with them.

Staff at institutions are often activity-oriented. As a rule, they try to help the residents at the institution to live an active life, and one of the methods they use to achieve this is often called *activation*. If by activation we mean the facilitation of activities and leisure arenas, this is an important method. But if by activation we mean arranging games that children and young people are persuaded to take part in, its positive and pedagogic value is more in doubt. It is true that this way of thinking can occasionally be useful, but, as a rule, adults ought to think of themselves more as facilitators and participants in play and less as having a responsibility to arrange games *for* the children. The educational element in play will probably come through regardless, and if it does not, playing still has a clear value in itself.

One activity with great social pedagogic potential is going on excursions. These could be short day trips or longer trips involving one or several overnight stays; in either case, it involves getting away from the everyday and humdrum. In this way, children and young people are given the opportunity to experience new things in different surroundings. Nearly everyone enjoys this. Such excursions also provide the social pedagogue with opportunities to manage situations that can be useful as new arenas for learning. Being tucked up in a sleeping bag under an open sky and talking until you fall asleep provides opportunities for linguistic actions completely different from everyday life at the youth club. Going to the beach with others from the school day-care club provides opportunities to meet new people as well as doing new things with people you already know. The opportunities offered by going on excursions are often especially useful for children or young people who are marginalised in daily life. Most trips involve relating to a reasonably sized group of people in a new and different environment.

Conflict, negotiation and the setting of boundaries

The social pedagogue's work with children and young people often involves conversations and discussions about scarce resources. Sometimes, this can be a shortage of economic resources ('I want more pocket money' or 'We cannot afford to buy expensive designer clothes'). Other times, the topic might be a shortage of time: 'Why are adults in meetings all the time?' or 'I cannot talk to you now, I have to talk to the other children as well'. This is not, of course, a situation that applies exclusively to these children and young people. In all families, family members need to negotiate on the distribution of things like money, influence, attention, involvement and so on. But children and young people who have had a difficult childhood, and perhaps especially those living away from home in foster families or residential facilities, probably experience this type of negotiation differently to those who grow up with their families.

In most families, the children are familiar with the codes for the distribution of benefits. They have learnt these codes through negotiation in innumerable situations from the very start. Such negotiations can be language-based, but not necessarily. One example of the latter is when one of the parents picks up a child and puts them on their lap. Normally, a sibling would not have a problem with this. But if he or she feels a bit lacking in attention for some reason, the natural thing would be to 'claim one's right', for example, by climbing up on the other side. Both the climbing into the lap and the parental reaction to this are elements in the negotiation. Children who negotiate in this way in their own families have more or less the same negotiation partners during their whole childhood. They know very well what is needed to get what they want.

On the other hand, children and young people who are placed outside the home must, as a rule, create their own negotiation practice and their own negotiation history. This implies trying to work out what is required to get access to what are often experienced as scarce resources, and also, at the same time, that these negotiations have to be held with many people they do not know. This is where the question of fairness is raised as an important aspect of the negotiation. A healthy social pedagogic environment has the means to handle this negotiation process. It is important to understand that attempts should not be made to 'administer away' such negotiations, for example, by setting up long lists of rules for solving all dilemmas. Negotiating is also hard work for the person responsible for the distribution of money, attention and benefits. The easy option is to try to avoid it. One important social pedagogic choice, therefore, is to ensure that such negotiations take place. Negotiation has a value in itself. It offers important opportunities for learning and development.

Another way to throw some light on this is to point out that conflict between the social pedagogue and the children and young people he works with can be seen as a resource. According to Larsen (1996), it is very important that what he calls 'the institution' deals with situations where clients demonstrate resistance to their treatment. The opposite of dealing with such situations can be described as trivialising them, or trying to cover up any disagreement. Translated into a social pedagogic understanding, we could say that the social pedagogue must deal with situations where the client is resisting change-oriented work.[2] Dealing with such situations is a core factor in social pedagogic practice. What happens in such situations is that, at best, the client can move forward – if they are handled well. Conflicts often clarify things that need to be clarified. In a social pedagogic context, it is probably conflicts that arise and are played out in the social environment that more than anything can be regarded as useful. The learning material in such situations can be exploited to teach children and young people how to behave in social situations 'in real life'. This requires the adult to be able to regard the conflict material as a resource (Larsen, 1994). This view is shared by Skau (2005, p 104), who writes that a dynamic and change-oriented understanding lead to us 'stress that conflicts are necessary and natural phenomena in connection with growth and development'. Conflicts sometimes arise when children and young people do not want the same things as the adults. In such a situation, the adult has three choices in the main: he can make a decision that goes against what the child wants; he can make a decision to go along with what the child wants; or he can enter into a negotiation with the child about which decision should be made. The social pedagogue practitioner ought to have all these three strategies in his action repertoire. It is difficult to generalise about when each of these three alternatives should be used. Sometimes, one will be right; at other times, another. It is the social pedagogue's reflective attitude and practice that will help him to arrive at the choice he thinks is the best in each individual situation. Conflict situations present a challenge for him both as a person and as a professional.

Good adult functions that the conscious social pedagogue ought to practise are: firmness; the willingness to negotiate; the ability to compromise; and the ability and will to resolve situations that have gridlocked. With the latter, I mean situations that cannot move forward regardless of what is said. The more pressure you put on the child or young person, the more he resists. We can talk about a force–counter-force situation. This requires a very strong will to focus on what is locked, without consideration for the personal prestige often invested in the preceding phase when force–counter- force was turning into gridlock. It is precisely in the build-up to such situations that these interventions are most useful. Force–counter-force situations are often emotionally charged. One competency that the social pedagogue can practise for use in such situations is listening. He should listen to the child/young person and to himself – to the arguments on both sides. This will help him to take a rational, balanced view and possibly reduce the risk of acting on a purely emotional basis.

The problem with the client resisting change-oriented work is superficially dealt with by several authors. In my view, Parton and O'Byrne (with reference to several authors; see 2000), for example, do not delve sufficiently deeply into the thematic structure when they claim that there is no resistance; that this really is only about the professional's lack of flexibility, or his failure to do the right thing in other ways. The proposed solution is to get better at forging alliances with the client. I perceive this as a morally based standpoint that has not been sufficiently investigated. I would suggest a closer investigation of the alliance between the social pedagogue and the client, looking at it from a communication and cooperation perspective. It may seem paradoxical to talk about cooperation when the problem is that clients sometimes resist cooperation. I still claim that it is meaningful, because it is not possible to resist cooperation if one is not invited to cooperate. When the social pedagogue invites cooperation, the client is given the opportunity both to cooperate, to resist cooperation and to alternate between the two. Inherent in this is a potential for development.

If we think about the alliance between the social pedagogue and the client as a collaborative alliance, it can be divided into two parts: one is a relationship part, the other a task part. The former is about the two people relating to each other on a personal level; and this puts certain demands on how they behave towards each other. The latter is about what they are to achieve on a more concrete level – which tasks they need to solve together. We can imagine straightaway that we are talking about a rational negotiation process. That is too simple, however. Real negotiation presupposes equal terms for both parties and complete agreement about what is to be negotiated. The alliance between the social pedagogue and the child or young person is mostly not like that. The asymmetric relationship between them means an unequal distribution between authority and responsibility. Besides, not all children and young people have arrived voluntarily at the client position. The concept of negotiation is still useful (Storø, 2001). It involves listening to the other person and presenting our own points of view.

At their best, the negotiations we are talking about here are very useful for children and young people. Children and young people with experience of child welfare services who learn negotiating skills in cooperation with adults manage better in adult life (cf Bieahl et al, 1995). But the negotiations are very complex. They consist of both what is known and what is unknown, they contain both rational and irrational elements, they are (as we have seen) both language-based and not language-based, and it is often difficult to get an overall view of all the events involved. Besides, it will often be the case that those participating in them (the child/young person and one or more social pedagogues) have different and changing opinions about them. The process of cooperation is constantly being constructed by those who participate in it. The same goes for the different actors' understanding of the cooperation process; the meaning they give to it. At the same time, understandings are constructed by other people who are in the vicinity and who are affected by the cooperation. These people give their constructions back to the cooperation, via the main actors. They may be, for example, the child's friends, parents or teachers. These constructions are complex social processes consisting of observation, interpretation, contribution and evaluation. There can be a multitude of reasons for cooperation problems. The picture is often so complex that it is impossible to point to a single, universal reason. But the social pedagogue's responsibility for driving the process forward forces him to delve into the situation and initiate fresh constructions. His client must be invited to participate actively in this process.

There is yet another clear advantage in constructing *cooperation with the client* as a main arena for the social pedagogue's practice. If we regard the client's resistance to change-oriented work as a breakdown in communication or in the cooperation process, we give ourselves opportunities to see the problem in terms of *the process*, and not *the individual*. This makes it easier to move forward than explaining the problems in terms of 'He is impossible to work with'. Cooperation presupposes reasonable agreement about goals, working methods and how to communicate. All these elements should be able to withstand continuous assessment from both the client and the social pedagogue. The collapse of one of the factors, such as the agreement on *how* communication should happen, could be interpreted as the breakdown of the whole cooperation. There is a danger that the client might be blamed for this – and that it would be interpreted as resistance. In such breakdown situations, therefore, it is important that the social pedagogue is prepared to root out the element that constitutes the problem, and that he invites cooperation in order to solve the problem. This would prevent a morally based interpretation of the breakdown.

These days, we often have a difficult relationship with the concept of setting boundaries. Many perceive it as belonging to the parenting of a previous era. Today, we encourage our children, we do not set boundaries for them. Raundalen (2004) goes as far as saying that he wants to abolish the concept, because in his view it is:

> a very poor and imprecise concept which gives very mistaken associations, namely that children simply allow themselves to be directed from the outside, by boundaries and the people who set them. The aim of upbringing should instead be to promote the empathic, controlled, internally-directed individual who assumes responsibility for his own actions.

Instead, he introduces the concept of 'confrontational learning', which implies 'grasping the unpleasantness of the situation and confronting the child face to face, because you want to establish a learning effect which reduces or prevents a repetition' (Raundalen, 2004). One central point in what the psychologist Raundalen writes is of interest to the topic of this book. He stresses the pedagogical element as that which distinguishes between what is good and what is less good. He also advocates the need for children to learn, but says that they learn better through confrontation than through the setting of boundaries.

One picture of what has happened to upbringing in our time is found in Dale (2006), who writes that a particular problem in postmodern upbringing is indulgence. The dissolution of rigid norms for bringing up children can lead to adults abdicating from the demand of showing authority. One of the reasons why we shy away from conflict in the upbringing of children could be that we are led by the images of what Dale (2006, p 38) calls 'the anti-authoritarian ideology of the 1970s'. According to Dale, upbringing includes three different actions: guidance, assessment and sanctioning. Of these, sanctioning is the action that is mostly associated with unpleasantness. It is, however, essential in order to be able to impart knowledge and skills for distinguishing between acceptable and unacceptable behaviour.

Others have introduced different concepts, for example, Vatne (2006), who writes about *the correcting perspective*. Vatne is more positive towards the concept of boundary-setting, and includes it as a method within milieu therapy. The setting of boundaries and correction are different phenomena. Setting a boundary implies saying 'This far, but no further'. The boundary that is set does not include any guidance beyond marking the outer limit of what is acceptable. A correction is more of a road map. When the adult corrects, he has the opportunity to build in an expectation that the child should choose a different behaviour. This can be communicated as a direct expectation, or as a relational expectation.

Grete is a milieu therapist in a residential home for young people. When she spots Charlotte walking into the common room wearing muddy boots, she says: "Please don't go inside with those boots." She has set a boundary. Charlotte is in no mood

to listen to her, and carries on. Grete says: "Take your boots off when you are inside."
Again, Charlotte chooses to ignore her. Grete then goes up to Charlotte and says:
"When you walk into the common room with those boots the floor gets dirty. I
have washed the floor today, so I'd like you to help me to keep it clean. Please could
you take off your boots?"

In this example, we can see that Grete first uses a boundary-setting statement;
then she tries to correct the behaviour she sees; finally, she corrects in a way that
also gives an explanation of why she is correcting and that points out a relational
dimension between her and Charlotte. We can also place her second attempt at
stopping Charlotte in the category of confrontational learning. In practice, these
two live side by side. In some situations, such as when the child is exposed to
danger, it is right to set clear and indisputable boundaries. In other situations, the
social pedagogue will often try to include an educational and relational element, as
is shown particularly in the final statement here. In this statement, Grete introduces
an element of negotiation at the same time as establishing an expectation about
what she wants Charlotte to do. In this language-based action, she shows that she
would like Charlotte to both remove her boots and contribute to the community
and the relational exchange between the two of them.

The different types of boundary-setting, confrontation and correction are ways
to teach children and young people the difference between right and wrong. We
could say that we are teaching the children rules, but also that we are teaching
them about the culture we live in. Both these educational projects are well-
placed within a social pedagogic framework. Most, if not all, rules and norms are
culturally determined. Therefore, teaching children what is acceptable and what
is not in the culture we inhabit means giving them useful tools for eventually
having to manage life on their own. Mastering the culture we inhabit is one of
the fundamental elements of social pedagogic theory (cf Madsen, 2006).

One specific reason why we are reluctant to use the concept of boundary-
setting these days is probably that we often focus on what Sandbæk (2004) calls
the actor status of children. This implies understanding children as active creators
of their own reality, which is in line with social constructionist thinking. We are
interested in the *exploring* child rather than the *child who needs upbringing*. But it is
important to reflect on new ways of thinking. Madsen (2006) and Sandbæk (2004)
warn against some of the consequences of the understanding of the active child
that is provided by modern childhood sociology. Children also need protection,
and this implies adults' responsibility to give guidance. This is just what a social
pedagogic perspective does, giving provisions for upbringing, and elevating this
concept to a fundamental one in the relationship between children and adults
(Mathiesen, 2008).

In a social pedagogic professional context, we can understand boundary-setting
and structuring as parts of the learning process towards the future goal of being
able to manage on one's own. Gaining knowledge about what is customary

within a culture is necessary in order to enable participation in a community. When individuals enter into a community, they are put to the test when it comes to discovering the governing norms and rules of the community and following them. Norms and rules regulate behaviour, but so do verbal utterances for example. The community accepts certain types of behaviour and certain statements, and not others. By setting boundaries, correcting and confronting each other, the individuals in a community build a culture that provides knowledge about what leads to inclusion – as well as marginalisation. In the adult–child relationship, boundary-setting, correction and confrontation are contributions to upbringing into a community. Social pedagogues who use boundary-setting methods sometimes revert to learning-oriented theory in order to underpin their actions. This is particularly seen in the method *token economy*, which is about giving clear positive and negative reinforcement for the behaviour of children and young people through a reward system, where they can earn points to be exchanged for various benefits. For some, this is an effective learning method, while others perceive the sole concentration on external behaviour as problematic.

It is important to thematise the dilemmas of boundary-setting. One dilemma is that the setting of boundaries can turn into a mechanical use of force. Another touches on the force element in boundary-setting: unreasonable boundaries also imply the unreasonable use of force. On the other hand, the absence of boundaries and correction is also a problem. We can say that the social pedagogue's upbringing responsibility means that he has to deal with both boundary-setting and correcting functions, *and* give the child the opportunity genuinely to have experiences he can call his own. Vatne (2006) writes about finding a balance between correction and acknowledgement. We could also say that the social pedagogue must be able to confront and sanction in an authoritative way, but without offending the child or young person (cf Kreuger, 1986a, 1986b; Larsen, 2004). On the contrary, children and young people should, as a result of their upbringing, be given the opportunity to expand their own rationality in a dialogic meeting with the upbringing authority (Dale, 2006).

Lastly in this section on boundary setting, it might be useful to mention what some perceive as the opposite, namely, a pleasant atmosphere and encouragement. I would argue that these are not really contrasts. As I see it, children will perceive a balance between what is encouraging and what is boundary-setting/correcting as reasonable. For the social pedagogue, this way of thinking demands a broad range of attitudes and skills. A reminder of Løvlie Schibbye's (2009) concept of acknowledgement might be useful here. This implies seeing the other person as a subject. Acknowledgement in communication is sometimes put forward as an ideal; but, according to Bae (1988), acknowledgement is more than just a communication technique. It is about how you behave, about integrity in the relationship with the other person. We can say, therefore, that boundary-setting and correction ought to be carried out in a climate where the intervention can be understood as part of a subject-oriented attitude, and not as the only content of a relationship.

It is quite common to perceive the balance between boundary-setting and acknowledgement/encouragement as 'Having to say "yes" 10 times for each "no"'. This statement is based on an attitude of learning theory that believes in the necessity of more positive than negative reinforcements. But we can also regard it as an ethical rule of the road that says we should strive to behave in a positive way towards the other person. When we do intervene, the other person will perceive the intervention as something other than technical and interfering, making it easier to regard it as a necessary part of a positively oriented adult–child relationship.

Mealtimes

In institutions and other arenas where the social pedagogue practises his profession, mealtimes are often regarded as central to the social pedagogic activity. Mealtimes are for the intake of nutrition, but, of course, also a lot more. Residents and staff of an institution get together for meals. We can say that a meal has three main functions in the social pedagogic sense: food, socialising and conversation.

Some may think it odd that I even mention food in connection with mealtimes. Obviously, people will eat. What has that got to do with social pedagogy? Surely, the other things we do while eating are more interesting from a social pedagogic angle? I would say that it is not as simple as that. First, the food itself is important. Some who become clients of the social pedagogue are not very good with the whole food thing. They are not used to enjoying food by themselves or with others, and they are not always eating the right food and the right amount of food. The last point concerns those who eat too much or too little, but also those who eat nutritionally poor food. We know, for example, that too much sugar makes children restless.

Second, food is important through its function in the client's (and everybody else's) everyday life. Eating is a straightforward non-technical everyday activity. Food is important to the social pedagogue precisely because it is *not* about his profession. It is important to include aspects other than the explicitly professional when spending time with clients, and for the clients, it is important to be able to do something other than just talk. It is quite common among social pedagogues to regard mealtimes as an opportunity to bring together clients and those who work with them. Perhaps this is based on an old extended family ideal, translated, for example, into institutions, where they make sure that such communal mealtimes are arranged every day. In many places, this is the most important single point in the structure of the institution, not unlike the way many families with children regard mealtimes in their hectic everyday lives. Gathering round the table for a meal is one of very few everyday rituals left in Norwegian culture in our time. Norwegian culture is changing, not least because many people with a different cultural background have moved to the country; but, looking at the big picture, we can assume that this particular everyday ritual has not changed much. When we talk about ritual, we touch on something that has to do with the social pedagogic perspective. Ritual has many aspects, but I will only mention one of them here. Ritual represents the security of the constantly recurring. This is an important function to bring into social pedagogic everyday life. By giving children and young people recurring experiences over time, we help them to lead more complete lives.

Another important aspect of mealtimes is the conversations round the table. I have written about conversations earlier and will therefore not dwell much on them here. I would just like to mention that there may be a danger in social pedagogical contexts of turning the conversation during the meal into a 'pedagogical' one. What I mean is that we should stop and think before making mealtime conversations planned and goal-oriented. We could, of course, say that social pedagogy is much more than just goal-oriented; indeed, that is one of the fundamental ideas in this book. But there is, nevertheless, good reason to warn against abusing the meal by turning it into a meeting rather than an informal gathering. There is always a lot to talk about in the everyday life of social pedagogues and clients. Mealtimes ought to be disconnected from the most goal-oriented of such conversations.

A rest from development and change-oriented work

With this, I have set the agenda for the next section, where I shall briefly turn to a very important aspect of social pedagogic practice. When children and young people are exposed to the social pedagogue's change-oriented work, there is always a danger that the change orientation overshadows other aspects of the relationship. Not doing anything *can* be perceived as being passive. 'Doing nothing' while in the vicinity of a social pedagogue could be interpreted as not being receptive to development. Upbringing is inherent in the social pedagogic project, while resting is less clearly expressed as a theme.

Personal development and change can be regarded as work, which leads to the person engaged in it becoming tired. In other contexts, such as when doing physical work, it is normal to build in rest periods. There is seldom a need to campaign for this. But when the client is doing internal and external development work, the need for a rest does not appear to be acknowledged in the same way. The social pedagogue can compensate for this by including breaks and recreational opportunities in the daily structure. It ought to be just as natural to arrange certain periods *without* clear learning targets as arranging periods *with* such targets. In a holistic way of thinking, these interim periods will also present clear social pedagogic opportunities, starting with 'everyday' interaction with the client. The interim periods can also be used as a reward for the client's work: 'You have worked really hard to move forward, let's take it easy for a few days, you have deserved it.'

Local methods

When the social pedagogue works with children and young people, he has certain general methods at his disposal; which I have shown some examples of in the preceding section. In addition, there are other, not so general, methods. These are local, and linked to certain contexts. Some would argue that they cannot really be called social pedagogic methods or tools, but rather 'good ideas'. That does not mean that they are less important. Practitioners in all professions often find good means to solve problems in a particular way. This is where the special strength of the practitioner lies. Whether we are talking about a carpenter, a dentist, an actor or a social pedagogue, he will develop his practice in the light of his experience. When I give some examples of such distinctly local concepts and strategies in this book, it is partly just to demonstrate them, because I think they are very useful. It is also to show examples of how social pedagogic practice can be developed locally.

I shall describe some of the good strategies I myself have learnt and helped develop in places where I have worked.[3] My examples all stem from residential homes for young people, but they could also have occurred elsewhere. Readers with a certain experience from professional practice will recognise some of this. Similar measures may have been developed in other places, and been given other names. Some measures are never formulated, as I am doing now. Sometimes, they are formulated orally, often in a local context between colleagues at the same workplace.

The wheelhouse conversation

My first suggestion for a useful measure is what I have learnt to call *wheelhouse therapy*. In order to cultivate a social pedagogic way of thinking (rather than a psychological one), I have chosen to call it *the wheelhouse conversation*. If I were to give this phenomenon a theoretical formulation, it would have to be something like this: the wheelhouse conversation is a type of conversation between two participants – the social pedagogue and the client – who are standing or sitting next to each other and looking in the same direction. In this conversational mode, they are alternating between talking about the client's experiences and completely different topics.

The concept was originally developed by Morten Hansen, the skipper of the boat that was part of the school and work facilities at the institution. Over a long period, he observed that standing together in the wheelhouse with a youngster holding the wheel and watching the force of the ocean provided completely different opportunities for togetherness and conversation from what could be expected in arranged social pedagogic conversations. The conversations in the wheelhouse on the little boat – which sometimes had to fight its way through the waves in bad weather, and other times glided smoothly through calm waters with the morning dew still on the deck – were of a different type to those occurring in different situations. Here, he found that he was getting closer to each individual youngster despite the aim of such conversations never being pedagogical – or maybe precisely because of it. Here, confidences and reflections were easily forthcoming without him having to ask for them. The explanation for what happened is probably quite simple. Standing in the wheelhouse on the boat, pedagogy or change-oriented work are not on the agenda. The most important thing is probably that this situation has *no specific* agenda. The absence of pressure to be part of change-oriented work may have opened the young people up to exactly one of the activities that characterises change-oriented work, namely, talking about it. In these situations, it was possible to reflect freely, and it would not be 'wrong' if the conversation moved on to other topics halfway through. The pressure to perform was minimal – as long as you steered the boat.

We see that the real theme of the situation is something other than pedagogic. You do not stand in a wheelhouse to talk; you stand there to steer the boat. It is exactly this doing something else together that contributes to giving the conversation such a positive slant. This can, of course, be exploited in numerous situations in all social pedagogic activity. You can go fishing, or shopping, you can watch TV, listen to music, stay together late into the night in the common room at the institution (and stay awake much longer than usual), and you can have a coffee. Exactly this last point – drinking coffee together – is something most of us do without necessarily having a purpose for the conversation that takes place while we are drinking the coffee. Nevertheless, many people would say that they have the best conversations over a cup of coffee.

Can we call it a social pedagogic conversation when it really was not planned as such? In my opinion, yes. Experience from social pedagogic practice shows that the really good solutions are sometimes found where you are not initially looking for them. As I mentioned in Chapter One, there can be an inherent danger of the pedagogue becoming 'too pedagogic'. I am, in other words, warning against an excessively strong pedagogic orientation in the execution of practice. The pedagogue can become his own worst enemy if he forgets the human, the immediate, dimensions of being a client. A clear orientation towards others can be useful in the social pedagogue practitioner's work. At the same time, we must not throw the professional perspective overboard. The social pedagogue who finds himself in 'wheelhouse-like' situations must bring his profession's theoretical understanding with him into the situation. Only then will he be able to exploit its potential. On the other hand, if he becomes too eager to intervene 'on the hoof', he may damage the situation and others like it. Some of the 'magic' in the situation can be broken, and may never return. The wise social pedagogue takes his time and assesses whether his feedback on the young person's reflections should be given at once, or maybe in another situation at another time. Sometimes, there may simply be no need for feedback, maybe it is enough that the 'third mate' (the social pedagogue) is listening.

Many social pedagogues with experience of working with children and young people have practised the wheelhouse conversation in various forms. The most obvious comparison is driving in a car with a child or young person. In the same way, this is a situation that invites a different kind of conversation to the strictly pedagogic. Staff at institutions have understood this. Sometimes, they use it as a method: taking a youngster who does not want to talk about himself on a car journey, or going for an evening drive with a young person you have an important message for. Driving while it is dark intensifies the 'wheelhouse feeling'.

It ought to be said that the last part of the original version of this concept, that is, 'therapy', needs to be understood from a certain ironic distance. Therapy is not, in itself, an arbitrary activity. It is facilitated, arranged and supported by one or several theoretical perspectives. The wheelhouse *conversation* is more a description of a situation that is 'arbitrary' in the sense that what happens is not planned (apart from steering the boat). Planning is limited to the staging: two people in the given context with an opportunity to talk freely and spontaneously.

Positive white lies

The second strategy I want to describe here is something I call *positive white lies*. Some would immediately ask what on earth can be social pedagogic about telling lies. And it also has to be said that this concept is loaded with a certain irony. It has never been intended as anything other than a very local expression among colleagues who are all very familiar with its meaning. As I am now taking the chance to spread it to a wider audience, I feel I need to provide a brief explanation.

As I remember it, the concept emerged between some colleagues who felt that they had observed something special. I can no longer recall who the actual originator was. The concept, which was formulated by a creative colleague, originates from experience of working with young people. The concept is about understanding learning as something more than just rote learning, for example, of arithmetical tables and historical dates. It is an expression of optimism for pedagogy.

Positive white lies are something else. They are about speaking something other than the truth, but 'for the good'. The most obvious example is when the social pedagogue says to a young person who cannot manage very effectively: 'You did really well there!' We often talk to young children in this way when they show us what they can do – it is easy for adults to exaggerate their praise in such situations. Doing this to young people who constantly show negative behaviour, and challenge those trying to help, is not as easy. In these cases, praise must be found elsewhere than in the immediate pleasure one can feel when a small child manages to use the potty for the first time.

Children and young people who have a difficult relationship with other people often also have a difficult relationship with their own achievements. They have mostly got used to managing without praise. Maybe because they know that they rarely get any. Perhaps because they feel little appreciated. In such cases, it may be a smart move to 'top up their account' with praise and positive feedback. Of course, the adult cannot go around praising everybody all day long in every thinkable situation. There must be real reasons for the positive feedback; if not, they will be seen as false. It is important, therefore, to give praise as soon as possible, and also to give it in a more positive way than the child or the young person really 'deserves' in relation to the skill shown. The social pedagogue who wants to reinforce positive behaviour in this way needs to be able to spot the nearly invisible glimmer of a good performance in the child or young person.

Being praised for something we have done is often a value-laden issue. Praise needs to be earned. This is an underlying contract in our culture, which is also strongly present in the meeting between the social pedagogue and the client. *Positive white lies* in such situations are, therefore, partly to exceed this cultural norm. The child or young person who normally never receives praise and therefore does not achieve, is made to believe that he has done something 'well enough'.

Positive white lies can only be used with a great deal of wisdom. It can easily become false and condescending to give higher praise than the child or young person deserves. The social pedagogue normally works best when he also tells the truth.

The Kjell syndrome

The *Kjell syndrome* is an interesting concept that is meant more as a self-critical comment to the social pedagogue practitioner than as a description of a method. The concept has a very concrete history. The event that gave rise to the syndrome has only happened once. But this led to a valuable professional insight that was used at the school for many years afterwards.

The event unfolded when Kjell (obviously not his real name) did not want to go to school. This happened over time. That is to say, he did go to school, but he did not sit in the classroom during lessons. Normally, he sat under some stairs without doing anything at all. Kjell did not have good experiences with being a pupil. He was constantly given confirmation of everything he did not know, and he felt that it was easier to live his everyday life under the stairs than at his desk. His teachers were despairing of the fact that they were unable to give the boy the education he needed and had a right to, and the milieu therapists also stepped in and tried to contribute with conversations and other initiatives. Kjell's parents were informed, and they were not very happy with the situation either.

Suddenly, one day, Kjell was at his desk at the start of the first lesson. His teacher was amazed, and could not help asking what had happened. Why had he come to school? Kjell's answer was very simple. He said: "Jan said I had to." Kjell gave this other teacher (Jan Tesli Stokke) credit for the change, and he is also the one who has been credited with the actual concept. What had happened? During the time Kjell had been sitting under the stairs, both his teacher, Jan, and the other teachers had time and again tried to make him come to lessons. They had tried in different ways: coaxing, tricking, talking about the consequences of not attending school, offering to help with schoolwork and so on. But Kjell stayed under the stairs. Gradually, the teachers realised that the boy needed time. They still made new attempts every day to get Kjell into the classroom, but they also ensured that the teaching continued as normal with the other pupils. When Kjell then suddenly turned up at his desk, he said it was because his teacher had said he had to.

The expression 'the Kjell syndrome' was developed during discussions among the teachers in the days following what happened. One of the topics of discussion was what had 'turned' Kjell. It might seem as if all the 'pedagogically correct' methods that the teachers had tried day after day had not had any effect. What, on the other hand, did seem to have managed to get Kjell back at his desk was a simple and straightforward message that he *had* to. Maybe it was just this simple message that worked. Maybe it was the case that Kjell felt a bit overwhelmed by all the good arguments from the adults, and couldn't find exactly what was needed for him to change his behaviour.

It was this effect that was given the name 'the Kjell syndrome'. The social pedagogue sometimes uses so many methods that he is in danger of getting lost in them. Sometimes, it may be better to try to keep it simple. In this case, it may have looked as if the boy was unable to relate to all the well-meaning suggestions, except to this one, timely, sentence. But this was probably not the case. It is far more probable that all the attempts to try to get him into the classroom had led to the situation where the simple thing succeeded in the end. After all, it was probably not just this one teacher, but all the teachers together, who had succeeded in getting Kjell back on track. The story about Kjell is still a reminder of what I wrote in Chapter One about the significance of acting 'non-pedagogically'.

I should add that Kjell subsequently continued to attend classes.

Holding the fort

Sometimes, things happen that threaten the structure of everyday life in an institution, or in other places where work goes on with children and young people. This could be both small and large crises. It could be young people acting out or escaping. Or it could be a child who does not turn up at supper because he is upset. In such cases, it is not uncommon for milieu therapists to drop everything (more or less literally) and run over to deal with what has happened. But this sometimes leads to completely new problems, and they are created by adults.

Of course, it is important that someone gets a grip on a crisis and tries to minimise it. If, for example, two children are fighting in the common room at the institution, they should usually be stopped. But interventions in such situations must be thought through. What often happens is that everyone at work does exactly the same thing: they 'put out fires'. This can be effective in order to put an end to the negative situation. But then what? What ought to happen straight after the fighting has been stopped? What about the other children who are present? What happens during the rest of the evening?

One important function in everyday life in an institution that is easily forgotten in such situations is what we might call taking care of the normal, everyday structure. The everyday structure has many good functions. A lot of time and effort have usually gone into planning and implementing it. It is usually seen as one of the most important aspects of an institution. At the same time, we see that it is precisely the everyday structure that is easiest to put to one side in situations where it is challenged. The concept of 'holding the fort' points to the importance of a quick return to the good, well-thought-out, everyday structure. This sends an important signal to the two who are fighting; by holding the fort, the milieu therapists are saying 'We have stopped you, but the world goes on.' It is important that these two do not have the experience of gaining a position of power in the community through fighting or other acting out. A quick return to everyday life is just as important for the other children who are present. For them, it is essential to feel that safety and predictability are quickly restored if something unpleasant occurs.

The function of holding the fort indicates that the basic values laid down by the institution are important, also in a crisis. These values are safety, predictability, adult control and recurring routines.

The talk little method

The *talk little method* may seem paradoxical. But, then, social pedagogic practice is not, at first glance, coherent and easily understood in all respects. It may seem paradoxical that I suggest talking little when I, at the same time, write that this practice must be understood as a language-based practice to a large extent. The *talk little method* is a warning to verbose social pedagogues that they can, at times, talk *too* much. Using too many words carries the risk of imprecision, and therefore difficulties in conveying the message. Besides, the talkative social pedagogue might be caught in another trap, one that is even more important to be aware of: he might dominate the conversation so that the client is unable to get a word in, or does not have time to think.

One way to imagine the *talk little method* in practice is when telling the client that what he did in a particular context was not good. In such situations, it is easy to say too much. Instead, it might be better to approach the child/young person and say what one has to say – and then walk away from the situation. That leaves the other person standing alone, and able to reflect.

When Anne-Grethe learnt that Christian had played truant again, she was exasperated and angry. She felt like giving him a proper piece of her mind so that he would really understand that this was no good. Instead, she chose to walk up to him and say: "I heard you skived off school today. That wasn't very clever." Then she turned on her heels and went over to the other youngsters who were playing volleyball at the back.

In this example, Anne-Grethe discovered both that her emotional reaction to what had happened could be useful as material in relation to Christian and that she was also in danger of overusing it. Therefore, she chose another solution:

producing a brief version, and then letting the boy himself work out what he wanted to do with it.

Later that evening, Christian came up to Anne Grethe. "Are you still angry with me, or what?", he asked. Anne-Grethe then chose to sit down with him and have a longer chat, where she explained a little more about what she had been thinking.

The *talk little method* can also be used as part of a greater communicative action that takes place over time. The two situations in the example demonstrate that the brief message in the first situation presumably had an effect on how the second situation played out. The intervening period between the two situations gave Christian the opportunity to reflect and to construct an understanding that he was then able to test on Anne-Grethe. When he approached her, Anne-Grethe understood that he was ready for a chat.

For me, this working method arises from what a colleague (Dan Brovold) once taught me, namely, that a pause is an important communication tool. It is during a pause that the message delivered to the other person is given a chance to sink in. It is only when you have finished talking, after a verbal full stop, that the client can begin to work out what he wants to do about the talk. If we are to believe that clients construct understandings based on their experiences, we have to allow them time and space in order to carry out this construction work.

The language-proficient social pedagogue can easily become patronising. He may try to show the client all his own thoughts about what happened, and demonstrate all the arguments for another way of doing things. The client rarely needs 'a complete encyclopaedia' of information about what the social pedagogue thinks. What he probably has a great deal more need for is a reaction to what he has done – maybe an emotionally charged reaction – and then time and space to review both his own actions and the reactions he got from the social pedagogue. If the reaction is what really counts, it needs to be fairly unambiguous. It can also successfully include an element of emotion: anger, pleasure, disappointment, frustration and so on. When the language-based feedback is accompanied by an emotional message, it will probably have a different effect to one delivered as a message stripped of emotional content. If we think of social pedagogic practice as a practice that promotes opportunities for learning in social situations, as I suggested at the beginning of this book, it is natural to assume that language and emotions are natural companions in situations involving social interaction.

It is important not to think about all encounters between the social pedagogue and client in this way, as brief conversations. Other times, we need to take our time and burrow deeper into the conversation. In some conversations, it is even natural for the social pedagogue to do most of the talking and for the child/young person not to be expected to do anything other than listen. I think Maier (1997) has a good point when he claims that young people need *endless talking sessions* with adults where they have opportunities to reflect on 'everything and everybody'.

Use of methods and strategies

I understand these types of 'local methods' as social constructions. They are negotiated during practice, while being carried out. According to Åberg et al (2001), social pedagogic practice is often very clearly locally based and linked to particular practice contexts. Because of this, they are often not shared by others. My descriptions of 'local methods' must be understood in this light. I have attempted to describe the local in such a way that others may discuss its global potential. Individual social pedagogues who read this must themselves decide whether the 'local methods' described here can be transferred to other practice situations. The specialist function of *adapting methods to the context where one works* is an important function. Social pedagogic practice is contextual and has to be tailored to the individuals in question. The social pedagogue, therefore, needs to look for methods and strategies that he can use at his own workplace. He can, for example, look at what skilful colleagues do in particular situations, and copy them. This is called 'learning from the master' (Schön, 2001). In this context, I am thinking about the so-called 'person-centred' type of learning from the master. Both this and the decentred type are mentioned by Nielsen and Kvale (2006), and they are both equally relevant in this context. The decentred type of learning from the master concerns the inexperienced person's learning by participation in a practice community, or social learning community, as Herberg and Jóhannesdóttir (2007) call it.

Notes

[1] For many children and young people who have been taken into care after resolutions by the Norwegian county social welfare board, the extent of home visits will be laid down in the resolution.

[2] I have mostly chosen to avoid the concept of resistance, as this is heavily anchored in psychological theory, particularly in the psychodynamic tradition. Instead, I have chosen to focus on the client's action, that is, resisting the social pedagogue's contribution.

[3] This is, first and foremost, about Grepperød Child Welfare Centre. This institution has always 'dared' to be innovative.

CHAPTER EIGHT

Afterword

This book began in a discussion between two people who both had a relationship with the concept of social pedagogy. While talking to each other, they did not immediately feel a connection. I hinted that this could be regarded as a picture of the complexity of the profession, but also as a crisis in the relationship between theory and practice. A chapter on theory followed, describing the social pedagogic profession as multi-theoretical. And here, many pages later, it ends with a description of practice.

It has been my hope to demonstrate some of the diversity of social pedagogic practice. It exists – as a practice – and interacts with a varied surrounding theoretical landscape. It is difficult to incorporate a description of social pedagogy between two covers of a book. But that does not mean that we should not try. Given more space, I could have gone further with a description of social pedagogic dilemmas. For social pedagogy is packed with dilemmas. It has to be, as it provides few clear answers. The right solution to a practical situation must always be negotiated by those who find themselves in the situation where the solution is to be applied. One of the dilemmas is in the relationship between the profession's increasingly louder demand for a theoretical base for action and the clients' need for a people-centred practice. Åberg et al (2001, p 39) point to the limits of 'how far professionalisation can meaningfully go'. At the same time, we must remember that the client has a right to a high professional level in the help he is exposed to. Åberg et al (2001, p 40) further point out that:

> the social pedagogic targets have changed from re-upbringing and normalising, to goals about activation, self-determination and quality of life…. Changes in the profession's view of itself and different demands from society paint a picture of an increased individualisation in the concrete work situation of social pedagogues with focus on each individual's pedagogic effort.

We can see that the current ideal of the individual also has an effect on social pedagogic practice. This presents a challenge to the theoretical foundation of this professional field.

We will probably see a further development of the theoretical concepts, as well as the practice itself, in the coming years. In recent years in Norway, social pedagogy has increasingly had the wind in its sails; and I hope that this book may contribute to developing the discussion further. In addition, I hope that it may contribute to good, well thought-out, practice.

Bibliography

Aamodt, L.G. (1997) *Den gode relasjonen – støtte, omsorg eller anerkjennelse?*, Oslo: Ad Notam Gyldendal.

Åberg, Å et al (2001) *Social pædagogikk og socialpædagogisk praksis i Norden.* København: Nordisk forum for socialpædagoger.

Album, D. (1996) *Nære fremmede. Pasientkulturen i sykehus*, Oslo: Tano.

Bae, B. (1988) 'Voksnes definisjonsmakt og barns selvopplevelse', *Norsk pedagogisk tidsskrift*, no 4.

Bastøe, P.Ø., Dahl, K. and Larsen, E. (2002) *Organisasjoner i utvikling og endring. Oppgaveløsning i en ny tid*, Oslo: Gyldendal Akademisk.

Berglund, S.-A. (2004) 'Det välgörandre med at uttrycka sig – socialpedagogik och narrativ metod i det moderna', in L. Eriksson, H.-E. Hermansson and Munger, A.-C. (eds) *Socialpedagogik och samhällsförståelse. Teori och praktik i socialpedagogisk forskning*, Stockholm: Brutus Östlings Bokförlag Symposion.

Biehal, N., Clayden, J., Stein, M. and Wade, J. (1995) *Moving on: young people and leaving care schemes*, London: HMSO.

Bisgaard, N.J. (2006) 'Pædagogiske teorier og dannelsesbegrebet', in N.J. Bisgaard and J. Rasmussen (eds) *Pædagogiske teorier*, Værløse: Billesø & Baltzer.

Bø, I. and Helle, L. (2002) *Pedagogisk ordbok*, Oslo: Universitetsforlaget.

Bronfenbrenner, U. (1979) *The ecology of human development. Experiments by nature and design*, Cambridge, MA: Harvard University Press.

Burr, V. (2003) *Social constructionism*, East Sussex: Routledge.

Dale, E.L. (2006) *Oppdragelse i det refleksivt moderne*, Oslo: Gyldendal Akademisk.

Durrant, M. (1993) *Residential treatment. A cooperative, competency-based approach to therapy and program design*, New York, NY: W.W. Norton & Company.

Eriksson, L. (2005) 'Teoriers betydelse för förståelsen av socialpedagogik', in E. Cedersund and L. Eriksson (eds) *Socialpedagogiken i samhället. Rapport från en nordisk forskningskonferens vid Linköpings universitet*, Campus Norrköping, 11–12 November 2004, Linköping: Linköpings universitet, rapport no 2.

Eriksson, L. and Markström, A.-M. (2000) *Den svårfångade socialpedagogiken*, Lund: Studentlitteratur.

FO (Norwegian Union of Social Educators and Social Workers) (2002) *Yrkesetiske retningslinjer for barnevernpedagoger, sosionomer og vernepleiere*, Vedtatt på kongressen 20–24 November, Oslo: Fellesorganisasjonen for barnevernpedagoger, sosionomer og vernepleiere.

Fransson, E. (1996) *Rom for jenteliv? En sosiologisk studie av relasjoner i en barnevernsinstitusjon*, Oslo: Barnevernets utviklingssenter, rapport no 3.

Freire, P. (1999) *De undertryktes pedagogikk*, Oslo: Gyldendal Norsk Forlag.

Frønes, I. (1979) *Et sted å være – et sted å lære. En bok om sosial læring og forebyggende miljøarbeid*, Oslo: Tiden Norsk Forlag.

Frønes, I. (2001) 'Skam, skyld og ære i det moderne', in T. Wyller (ed) *Skam. Perspektiver på skam, ære og skamløshet i det moderne*, Bergen: Fagbokforlaget.

Furuholmen, D. and Schanche Andresen, A. (2007) *Fellesskapet som metode*, Oslo: Cappelen Akademisk Forlag.

Garsjø, O. (2001) *Sosiologisk tenkemåte*, Oslo: Gyldendal Akademisk.

Garsjø, O. (2003) *Institusjonen som hjem og arbeidsplass – et bidrag til institusjonsfaglig kompetanse*, Oslo: Gyldendal Akademisk.

Gjertsen, P. (2010) *Sosialpedagogikk. Forståelse, handling og refleksjon*, 2nd edn, Bergen: Fagbokforlaget.

Gresham, F.M. and Elliott, S.N. (1984) 'Advances in the assessment of children's social skills', *School Psychology Review*, no 13, pp 292–301.

Grønvold, E. (1997) *Den systematiske arbeidsmodellen*, Notat: Høgskolen i Oslo.

Grønvold, E. (2000) 'Teorier for miljøterapeutisk praksis gjennom 50 år', in A. Hagqvist and B. Widinghoff (eds) *Miljöterapi : igår, idag och imorgon*, Lund: Studentlitteratur.

Gulbrandsen, L.M. (2006) 'Kulturpsykologiske tilnærminger til barns utvikling', in L.M. Gulbrandsen (ed) *Oppvekst og psykologisk utvikling. Innføring i psykologiske perspektiver*, Oslo: Universitetsforlaget.

Gustavsson, A. (2008) 'Vår tids socialpedagogik', in M. Molin, A. Gustavsson and Hermansson, H.-E. (eds) *Meningsskapande och delaktighet – om vår tids socialpedagogik*, Gøteborg: Daidalos.

Hämäläinen, J. (2005) 'Utmaningar i dagens urbana samhälle och socialpedagogik', *Sosiaalipedagoginen aikakauskirja*, vol 6, no 1, pp 27–38.

Hamburger, F. (2001) 'The social pedagogic model in the multicultural society of Germany', in L. Dominelli, W. Lorenz and H. Soydan (eds) *Beyond racial divides. Ethnicities in social work practice*, Aldershot: Ashgate.

Hegstrup, S. (2007) 'Hvem sætter agendaen for socialpædagogisk uddannelse?', *Social Kritik*, no 11, pp 52–66.

Helgeland, I.M. (2007) *Unge med alvorlige atferdsvansker blir voksne. Hvordan kommer de inn i et positivt spor?* Oslo: Unipub.

Henggeler, S.W., Schoenwald, S.K., Bourdin, C.M., Rowland, M.D. and Cunningham, P.B. (2000) *Multisystemisk behandling av barn og unge med atferdsproblemer*, Oslo: Kommuneforlaget.

Herberg, E.B and Jóhannesdóttir, H. (2007) *Kunnskap og læring i praksis. Fra student til profesjonell sosialarbeider*, Oslo: Universitetsforlaget.

Holst, J. (2005) 'Socialpedagogikkens udvikling i Danmark', in E. Cedersund and L. Eriksson (eds) *Socialpedagogiken i samhället. Rapport från en nordisk forskningskonferens vid Linköpings universitet*, Campus Norrköping, 11–12 November 2004, Linköping: Linköpings universitet, rapport no 2.

Howe, D. (1993) *On being a client: understanding the process of counselling and psychotherapy*, London: SAGE.

Jæger Sivertsen, K. and Kvaran, I. (2006) 'Sosialpedagogikken I Norge', in B. Madsen (ed) Sosialpedagogikk, Oslo: Universitetsforlaget.

Jansen, A. (2007) 'Om å skape seg selv og en fremtid. Betydningen av å fortelle historier', *Norges barnevern*, vol 84, no 4, pp 43–52.

Johanssen, J.C., Nygaard, M. and Schreiner, E. (1965) *Latinsk ordbok*, Oslo: Cappelen.

Kreuger, M. (1986a) *Careless to caring for troubled youth: a caregiver's inside view of the youth care system*, Washington, DC: CWLA Press.

Kreuger, M. (1986b) *Job satisfaction for child and youth care workers*, Washington, DC: CWLA Press.

Kunnskapsdepartementet (2005) *Rammeplan og forskrift for 3-årig barnevernspedagogutdanning.*

Kvale, S. (1997) *Det kvalitative forskningsintervju*, Oslo: Ad Notam Gyldendal.

Kvaran, I. (1996) *Miljøterapi. Institusjonsarbeid med children and young people*, Kristiansand: Høyskoleforlaget.

Langager, S. and Vonslid, W. (2007) 'Socialpædagogikkens genkomst', *Dansk Pædagogisk Tidsskrift*, vol 55, no 3, pp 3–7.

Langeveld, M. (1975) *Personal help for children growing up: the W.B. Curry lecture delivered in the University of Exeter on 8 November 1974*, Exeter: University of Exeter.

Larsen, E. (1992) *Miljøarbeid og arbeidsmiljø i barnevernets ungdomsinstitusjoner. Synspunkter på innhold og organisering*, Oslo: Barnevernets utviklingssenter, temahefte no 2.

Larsen, E. (1994) 'Læreren som rolle og ressurs i arbeid med ungdom som vil men ikke kan', in I. Helgeland (ed) *Arbeid med utfordrende ungdom i skolen*, Oslo: Kommuneforlaget.

Larsen, E. (1996) 'Service, behandling og samarbeid sett i et miljøterapeutisk perspektiv', in E. Larsen (ed) *Miljøterapeutiske temaer*, Oslo: SIR-gruppen.

Larsen, E. (2004) *Miljøterapi med barn og unge. Organisasjonen som terapeut*, Oslo: Universitetsforlaget.

Levin, I. (2004) *Hva er sosialt arbeid*, Oslo: Universitetsforlaget.

Lihme, B. (1988) *Socialpædagogik for børn og unge – et debatoplæg med særlig henblikk på døgninstitutionen*, Holte: SOCPOL.

Linde, S. and Nordlund, I. (2006) *Innføring i profesjonelt miljøarbeid. Systematikk, kvalitet og dokumentasjon*, Oslo: Universitetsforlaget.

Lundby, G. (1998) *Historier og terapi. Om narrativer, konstruksjonisme og nyskriving av historier*, Oslo: Tano Aschehoug.

Madsen, B. (2005) *Socialpædagogik og samfundsforvandling. En grundbog*, København: Hans Reitzels forlag.

Madsen, B. (2006) *Sosialpedagogikk*, Oslo: Universitetsforlaget.

Maier, H.W. (1997) *Barn og ungdom utenfor familien. Utviklingsmuligheter*, Oslo: AdNotam Gyldendal.

Manger, T (2005) 'Biprodukt av modernisering', in P.L. Brunstad and T. Evenshaug (eds) *Å være voksen*, Oslo: Gyldendal Akademisk.

Mathiesen, R. (1999) *Sosialpedagogisk perspektiv*, Hamar: Sokrates.

Mathiesen, R. (2008) *Et sosialpedagogisk perspektiv på individ og fellesskap*, Oslo: Universitetsforlaget (manus under utarbeidelse).

Myhre, R. (1982) *Hva er pedagogikk?*, Oslo: Gyldendal Norsk Forlag.

Nerdrum, P. (1997) 'Hvor god er den gode relasjon?', in B. Rappana Olsen and V. Bunkholdt (eds) *Barnevernet – mangfold og mening*, Oslo: Tano.

Nielsen, K. and Kvale, S. (2006) 'Mesterlære som læringsform', in N.J. Bisgaard and J. Rasmussen (ed) *Pædagogiske teorier*, Værløse: Billesø & Baltzer.

Nybø, L. (1999) *Aktiviteter og aktivisering i sosialpedagogisk arbeid*, Oslo: Pedkolon.

Nyqvist, L. (2004) 'Ungdomarnas konstruerandre av våld. Ett socialpedagogiskt perspektiv', in E. Cedersund and L. Eriksson (eds) *Socialpedagogiken i samhället. Rapport från en nordisk forskningskonferens vid Linköpings universitet*, Campus Norrköping, 11 –12 November 2004, Linkøping: Linköping suniversitet, rapport no 2.

Ogden, T. (1995) *Kompetanse i kontekst. En studie av risiko og kompetanse hos 10- og 13-åringer*, Oslo: Barnevernets utviklingssenter, rapport no 3.

Ogden, T. (1997) 'Risiko, sosial kompetanse og forebyggende arbeid i skolen', in K.J. Klepp and E. Aarø (eds) *Ungdom, livsstil og helsefremmende arbeid*, Oslo: Universitetsforlaget.

Oppedal, K. (2007) 'Kulturpsykologi og verdier – et etisk og danningsteoretisk perspektiv på menneskets sjelsliv', in O.H. Kaldestad (eds) *Grunnverdier og pedagogikk*, Oslo: Fagbokforlaget.

Parton, N. and O'Byrne, P. (2000) *Constructive social work. Towards a new practice*, Basingstoke: Palgrave.

Payne, M. (1991) *Modern social work theory. A critical introduction*, London: The Macmillan Press.

Raundalen, M. (2004) 'Overgrep mot barn på barnehjem og spesialskoler. Noen refleksjoner om hvordan det kunne skje, og om hvilken beredskap vi trenger for at det ikke skal skje igjen', Vedlegg 4 til NOU 2004:23, Barnehjem og spesialskoler under lupen, Oslo: Barne- og familiedepartementet.

Reichelt, S. (2006) 'Veiledningsgrupper med reflekterende team' in H. Eliassen, and J. Seikkula, (eds) *Reflekterende prosesser i praksis: klientsamtaler, veiledning, konsultasjon og forskning*, Oslo: Universitetsforlaget.

Røkenes, O.H. and Hansen, P.-H. (2006) *Bære eller briste. Kommunikasjon og relasjon i arbeid med mennesker*, 2nd edn, Bergen: Fagbokforlaget.

Sævi, T. (2007) 'Den pedagogiske relasjonen – en relasjon annerledes enn andre relasjoner', in O.H. Kaldestad (ed) *Grunnverdier og pedagogikk*, Oslo: Fagbokforlaget.

Sandbæk, M. (2004) 'Barn i hjelpeapparatet – kompetente og sårbare aktører', *Nordisk sosialt arbeid*, no 2.

Savater, F. (1997) *Mod til at opdrage*, København: Forum.

Schön, D. (2001) *Den reflekterende praktiker. Hvordan professionelle tænker når de arbejder*, Århus: Klim.

Schibbye, Anne-Lise Løvlie (2009) *Relasjoner. Et dialektisk perspektiv på eksistensiell og pskykodynamisk psykoterapi*, Oslo: Universitetsforlaget.

Skau, G.M. (2003) *Mellom makt og hjelp. Om det flertydige forholdet mellom klient og hjelper*, Oslo: Universitetsforlaget.

Skau, G.M. (2005) *Gode fagfolk vokser. Personlig kompetanse i arbeid med mennesker*, Oslo: Cappelen Akademisk Forlag.

Storø, J. (1997) 'Må være voksen', *Barne-og ungdomsarbeideren*, no 3.

Storø, J. (1999) 'Barneverninstitusjonen i framtida', *Nordisk sosialt arbeid*, no 4.

Storø, J. (2001) *På begge sider av atten. Om ungdom, barnevern og ettervern*, Oslo: Universitetsforlaget.

Storø, J. (2003) 'Det problematiske brukerbegrepet. En undersøkelse av et konkret møte mellom språk, politikk, vitenskap og faglig praksis i barnevernet', *Embla*, no 3.

Storø, J. (2005) 'Gullklumper i sanden. Ressursfokuserte og nettverksorienterte tilnærminger i arbeid med ungdom i institusjon', in L. Schelderup, C. Omre and E. Marthinsen (eds) *Nye metoder i et moderne barnevern*, Bergen: Fagbokforlaget.

Storø, J. (2008) 'Exit from care – developing a perspective', *Journal of Comparative Social Welfare*, vol 24, no 1, pp 13 –21.

Storø, J. (2012) 'The difficult connection between theory and practice in social pedagogy', *International Journal of Social Pedagogy*, vol 1, no 1, pp 17-29.

Vatne, S. (2006) *Korrigere og anerkjenne. Relasjonens betydning i miljøterapi*, Oslo: Gyldendal Akademisk.

Williams, F., Popay, J. and Oakley, A. (1999) 'Changing paradigms of welfare', in F. Williams, J. Popay and A. Oakley (eds) *Welfare research: A critical review*, London: UCL Press.

Wivestad, S.M. (2007) 'Hva er pedagogikk?', in O.H. Kaldestad, E. Reigstad, J. Sæther and J. Sæthre (eds) *Grunnverdier og pedagogikk*, Bergen: Fagbokforlaget.

Index

Note: the letter f following a page number indicates a figure and n an endnote.